Praise for *Does Your Life Need a Laxative?*

"Fred has captured the same dynamic, down-to-earth style and practical content in this book as he has given in his presentations on our ship. A real thought-provoking experience."

—Jay Gosselin, Assistant Cruise Director,
Holland America Cruise Lines

"The impact of Fred's message is so powerful and valuable that I have ordered 100 copies of the book as gifts for my clients and friends."

—Michael Pittas, Managing Director,
Pittas Foods, London, England

"This book kept my attention, made me think and I was moved to take some positive actions. I would definitely recommend it to those I care about."

—Charles Potok, President,
Companion Property and Casualty Group

"The book is a very enjoyable read. It contains many ideas on how to improve your outlook and your life. Fred put a lot of core principles for increasing one's happiness and improving one's relationships into perspective."

—Carolyn Halpern Oppenheimer, Executive Vice President,
Halpern Enterprises

"The *medicine* in this book is easy to swallow, is extremely practical, and most assuredly will make you, your life and your relationships happier. Dr. Fred understands how to connect with the reader; you will smile and be glad you took the time to read this book. Dr. Fred's "prescriptions" are sound advice worthy of following."

—Gregory Smith, Ph.D., President,
Executive Human Resource Solutions, LLC

"In this book, Fred really keeps your attention and makes you feel like he's having a one on one conversation with you. I was truly inspired and I was reminded that I have more control over my life and my happiness than I was using."

—Ed Quinones, President,
Aaron Rents

"I find Fred's book "guilty" of providing a wonderful blueprint for making one's life and relationships happier and more fulfilling. My "ruling" is that anyone interested in achieving this goal should definitely read it."

—Judge Jeryl Rosh

"This book should be a must read for people of all ages and backgrounds. I appreciate the importance and difficulty involved in motivating and teaching people to reach for their potential. Dr.Fred knows how to touch the right "buttons" and help the reader to progress on that journey."

—Anthony Trombetta, Director Of Sales
International Sanitary Supply Association

DOES YOUR LIFE NEED A LAXATIVE ?

Dr. Fred's

PRACTICAL PRESCRIPTIONS FOR HAPPINESS

FRED BRODER, Ph.D.

Fred Broder

NEW OUTLOOK PRESS

Published by New Outlook Press
5369 Seaton Way
Suite B
Atlanta, GA 30338

Cover and book design by Jill Balkus, www.jilllynndesign.com
Author photograph by Duane Stork Photography, www.dstork.com

ISBN-13: 978-0-9786-8750-2
ISBN-10: 0-9786875-0-7

Library of Congress Control Number: 2006906563

Printed and bound in the United States of America.

1 3 5 7 9 10 8 6 4 2

To purchase additional copies, please contact Fred Broder:
(770) 392-0382
fred@fredbroder.com
www.fredbroder.com

Contents

Dedication

How many of us get the opportunity to publicly acknowledge and thank those people who made a significant difference in our lives? The answer is that such opportunities are typically reserved for actors who stand up to accept an Oscar or Emmy, athletes who win Super Bowls and people who get business, social or community awards.

Well, since my acting skills are limited, I'm still working on my dunk shot and I haven't distinguished myself as a social activist, I realized that, for me, the best avenue to take that would allow me to thank the special people in my life was to write a book. So, for me, this Dedication section holds as much meaning as any chapter in this book. The philosophy that permeates the book is a reflection of the impact these people have had on me.

Let me begin with my parents, Sylvia and Herb Broder. As we know, whom we get as biological parents is an accident of birth. I was one of those very lucky people who hit the lottery. I could not have asked for more supportive, loving parents, who instilled in me an appreciation for people and their differences. Whatever compassion, sensitivity and humor I exhibit, I owe to those two wonderful people, who left an indelible imprint on my heart. My mom's daily encouragement and my dad's guiding spirit were both a true inspiration to me. My only regret is that my dad did not live to read this, my first book.

As I continually tell my children, one of the most important decisions they will ever make in their lives, should they choose to marry, is their selection of a mate. After thirty-three years of marriage to my best friend, my confidante, my lover, my dancing partner, my traveling companion and my soul mate, Glenda, I am more convinced than ever of the truthfulness of that statement. Glenda has given me the freedom, support, encouragement and confidence to pursue my career and the writing of this book. She has made daily sacrifices so that I could chase my dreams. Any success that I have only has meaning because I have Glenda at my side.

Just as in horse racing, I have been the winner of the "Triple Crown." Our three children—Eric, Jordy and Shira—each put the twinkle in my eye, the spring in my step and the pride in my heart. They are my "dream team." Glenda and I have been blessed to have three such loving, fun and good people as our children.

So "Does *My* Life Need a Laxative?" Not when it comes to my family. All I need and ask for is the wisdom, health and a little luck to enjoy the blessings that have been bestowed on me.

Again, let me thank my parents, my wife and my children for having the patience with, love for and confidence in this guy from the Bronx who believes he can help others improve their lives.

Acknowledgements

A special thanks to the wonderful people who took the time and care to review this manuscript and to give me some very valuable, and honest feedback as well as a tremendous amount of encouragement: Elaine Tavani, Liz Lyons, Sunny Lubner, Sharon Sarnat, Nicole Calloway and Mindy Hyman.

To my editor extraordinaire, Mim Eisenberg, president of WordCraft, Inc. in Roswell, Georgia, thank you for all your great suggestions. You saved me from myself and helped me retain a writing style that is close to the way I speak.

To my wonderful graphic designer, Jill Balkus, thank you for your creative genius in designing and laying out this book.

To Duane Stork for taking such a wonderful cover photograph that conveys an image of youthfulness in the face of rapidly advancing age.

A special thanks to the thousands of people who have taken the time to attend my presentations and seminars and who have asked me the question, "When are you going to write a book?"

Well, here it is!

Introduction

So provocative titles *do* get your attention. Well, you are about to get some steak with this "sizzle." It has been my experience that millions of people purchase motivational books, attend motivational seminars and listen to motivational tapes and CDs because they feel that they are either treading water or are drowning in the often turbulent oceans of life. They are grasping for a life preserver to keep themselves afloat. They want to be better, do better, feel better or get better in one or more areas of their personal or professional life. Everyone is looking for the genie, the wizard, the good witch, the angel, mystic or guru who will cast on him a spell of happiness and contentment.

Well, you can stop looking. Your journey and search is over, or perhaps just beginning, depending on your perspective. Just find your closest mirror and take a good long, hard look at that reflection. *You* are the wizard, the genie, the angel, the good witch. You get the point!

You have the power to significantly improve your life. However, understanding and accepting responsibility for this power and knowing when and how to use it will ultimately determine the impact it will have on your attitude, relationships and total life experiences.

So how is this book intended as a "laxative" for your life? I am going to share with and remind you of some things that will help you to **purge, expel and cleanse** from your attitudinal mindset, your behavior repertoire and habits those things you think, say and do that are sabotaging you and driving you away from the very things you want, deserve, and are capable of having out of life.

If you think about it, your desires, wishes, hopes and dreams many times are not in sync with your commitment to make them happen. I am often reminded of this disconnect at some of my lectures. Prior to delivering a presentation, I make it a point to mingle and chat with members of the audience. I want to get a sense of what's on their minds and to take their emotional temperature. Invariably, someone will ask what "new" things am I going to teach him during my talk. My stock answer is that there is really nothing very "new" that has come down from Mount Sinai that I can share regarding the principles of effective living. What I want to do is to remind people of the things that they already know, through past experience or common sense, about themselves, others and life but which they fail to practice consistently, in every situation. **It is this inconsistency of application that causes you to run into problems in your relationships.**

It's a very interesting phenomenon how, we, as people, always want to look to someone else and not ourselves, some expert or professional to bring us the recipe, the formula, the quick fix that will dramatically and quickly improve our satisfaction with life. We tend to look outward for motivation, nutritional and dieting control, physical well-being, and spiritual and intellectual growth and fulfillment.

In response to that demand for external guidance and nourishment has come forth a legion of gurus, experts, authors and authorities who have flooded the bookstores with their definitive bon mots, who have opened up clinics, spas and exercise establishments and who have provided the TV and radio talk shows with a wide and plentiful assortment of guests. Who can blame these individuals, who in the true spirit of free enterprise and capitalism have acted quickly to cash in on American society's latest preoccupation with self? These entrepreneurs have nothing to be apologetic for, since they are merely responding to a demand, from a substantial segment of our population, for a new category of goods and services.

Even yours truly is cognizant of the biblical saying: "Let he who is without sin cast the first stone." Surely the act of writing this book and giving thousands of talks on the very same topic places me in that same category of entrepreneurs. The major difference, hopefully, between this book and others, is in a fundamental assumption that I make about you, the reader. That assumption is that you already are as knowledgeable as I, if not more so, about yourself, your life and making your life what you want it to be.

Vince Lombardi, the famous football coach of the champion Green Bay Packers, was known to start off each pre-season practice by assembling the team, holding up a football and saying, "Gentlemen, this is a football." Upon hearing that, you might think, "By uttering such a simplistic statement, isn't he insulting a team of professional football players who have just won a Super Bowl?" But when you reflect on what Coach Lombardi's point was, you realize he was saying that no matter how good you are or think you are, for consistent success and performance it is critical that you periodically revisit the basics.

Thus I will merely try to serve as a cattle prod to help you revisit the basics of good, common-sense living and relationships. Using *low voltage*, I want to shock, stimulate and motivate you to reconnect with those "principles of living" that you already know but for a variety of reasons are not practicing to the degree that you could. Perhaps by taking you down this "memory lane" we can together find a way to reconfigure the puzzle pieces of your life in such a way as to provide you with the beautiful, exciting finished picture of what your life should and could be.

Before proceeding on this nostalgic journey, I think it important for me to dispel any inflated impressions you may have regarding my ability, as your "tour guide," to apply, in my own life, all the ideas we will discuss. As you probably know, a definite gap exists between one's ability to understand something on an intellectual level and one's ability to translate that knowledge, in one's own life, into action on an emotional level.

Thus, though I may know what I should do in a given situation, yet I too may have trouble applying that knowledge. I say this not with the intent of diminishing your faith in me as your "tour guide" but rather to enhance your faith in me because I am acknowledging my own fallibility. Too often, presenters and writers in this field do not convey to their audience the fact that they are just like you: people struggling through each day, attempting to attain fulfillment and comfort. So, dear reader, let us both embark upon this path of improvement with the acceptance and recognition that we both do so on feet of clay.

This is not a "how-to" recipe book. It is a book intended to make you **Think! Think! Think!** It's arranged in short chapters, each culminating with a specific "Prescription." Each point is shared using a down-to-earth, practical story or analogy that is easy to grasp and which is intended to motivate you to **do something** with those ideas, skills or concepts that you feel are applicable to your situation. The read is easy, but the points are significant.

One additional suggestion on how to prepare for this fascinating and important journey through the ideas discussed in this book: I recommend that, if at all possible, you read this only when you are totally alone in a very comfortable, quiet place where you are insulated from any human or mechanical distractions. It is really important that you allow yourself the luxury to concentrate, evaluate and think about what you are reading. This is not a novel in the sense that you will be reading and comprehending the trials, tribulations and triumphs of some fictitious characters that have been created to provide you with distraction and entertainment. Such novels can be read on a bus, train or in front of a blaring TV surrounded by three screaming children.

This book is a different kind of "novel." It is a review, an investigative journey into the inner recesses of your soul. It is, in short, a critique of your life, the novel entitled, *This Is Your Life*. What we will discuss is the character development, plot and unfinished chapters of the novel you have been living and developing since birth. Since your novel is still unfinished, it is important that you give it the attention it deserves. The best chapters are yet to come!

Please note that I have chosen to use the words "him" and "her" interchangeably in the different chapters of the book, rather than the more awkward "him/her" or "him or her" construction.

Two other important ingredients, humor and the use of analogies, have been liberally sprinkled throughout this book. If you were writing a recipe for your life, then humor would be an essential ingredient, akin to a spicy meat tenderizer that brings out the natural flavor of life while tenderizing or softening the toughness of living. Humor provides us with an acceptable escape or safety valve through which we can vent life's tensions while at the same time putting into perspective the inescapable realities of living. So when you periodically encounter an attempt at humor in this book, please accept it for what it is, a "tenderizer."

If selected wisely, analogies can help to crystallize in your mind a visual understanding of a thought or concept that might otherwise seem complicated or unclear. You will find many analogies in this book, which are used as vehicles to simplify a thought or principle of effective living.

When all is said and done, no book, speaker or set of tapes can dramatically improve your life on a day-to-day basis. **You and only you must take responsibility for making the changes that you feel are needed.** You can use this book as an attitudinal "laxative" to clear up some of your "fuzzy" or "toxic" thinking and behaviors that are currently interfering with your attainment of good health, more intense and qualitative happiness, success and satisfaction. Consider this book and prescriptions as the "antidote." Your personal Prescriptions for Happiness are now literally at your fingertips.

So let the cleansing begin!

CHAPTER 1

Don't Count Your Days, Make Your Days Count

(Note to reader: In this eulogy, please insert your name in the blank spaces below.)

"We are gathered here today to honor the memory and life of the late _____. _____'s untimely death has left all of his family, friends and all who knew him with a profound feeling of loss, for in reality there is no such thing as a "timely death." Regardless of how young or old one is when one dies, there is always a sense of unfinished business, unfulfilled dreams and unspoken words that those of us still alive wish we would have concluded or shared with _____ and that he has been denied attending to with us.

It is a trap of human nature to always assume that "there will be a tomorrow." We plan for the future, anticipating that things will be better. If we only remain patient, better health, more intimate love, greater happiness, professional fulfillment, financial security are all just down the road. The past is merely to be remembered for its impact on our present. Our present is merely to be viewed as a vehicle to our future. Our future is to be pursued as the answer to our prayers. The truth is that the past is gone and the future is elusive, not clearly defined, unpredictable and perhaps unattainable. However, the present *is the here and now*, which offers each of us, for better or worse, the greatest degree of control and direct, immediate feedback.

While deeply loved, appreciated and warmly remembered, _____ has now and forever been physically removed from our lives. We can no longer see, hear, touch, feel and interact with him. His Book of Life will have no new chapters to be written. The end has come. The loss, the hurt, the finality of his death must be fully comprehended and accepted, for none of us will be permitted another laugh, nor a tender touch, a smile, the shedding of a tear, the sharing of an idea nor the joys or disappointments of life with _____, nor he with us.

So as we bid farewell and lower _____'s casket into the ground, although it is too late for him, perhaps the living can in some way benefit from his death by looking for ways to stop counting each day on this earth but rather focusing on how we might make each day of our lives count. *Amen.*"

You and I have just been spectators at our own funeral. I must admit that it was an eerie experience for me to write , read and think about this eulogy. I suspect that as you injected your name into the eulogy, you may have had a similar experience. How did you feel about the thought that you had died? What were your emotions? How did you feel about the message in the eulogy?

It's been my experience that funerals are the times that

sober many of us up from a virtual stupor and the distorted way many of us live our lives. It's during the mourning of a departed friend or family member that we often ask ourselves, "What's life all about? Why am I here? What do I want? What's really important? How am I spending my time, and does it fulfill and satisfy my life?"

When we mourn, we reflect, we re-evaluate, we often re-commit or commit to do things differently, to be different, to act differently, to value differently. But these resolutions usually dissipate and evaporate within a few days or weeks after we leave the cemetery. We tend to return to that mindless path we were pursuing prior to attending the funeral.

Perhaps we were approaching most of our days as another chore to be endured. Our life seems, at times, to consist of a tedious, burdensome, almost unpleasant chain of activities that are regrettably necessary in order to attain that figment of our imagination called our "happier future."

We often treat each day of our life as if we are a prisoner in a penitentiary who marks off each day on the calendar wall of his cell as he counts down the conclusion of his sentence. Life should not be viewed or treated as a prison sentence. Relationships and experiences should not be taken for granted. To paraphrase a common saying, "Life on earth, your life, is not a dress rehearsal for the big show; it *is* the big show."

Imagine with me for a moment that this situation is real and that you are in fact being eulogized. Visualize those you love—your spouse, children, relatives, family, friends, colleagues—all standing by the gravesite crying, somber, mourning your passing. Their grief is profound. Then imagine that just before the lid on your casket is closed, somehow you are given a second chance. What would you do with that second chance? Whom would you want to see? What would you want to say? Where would you want to go? What would you like to do, feel or experience?

Frequently these are the questions that are given serious consideration and thought by people told by physicians that they only have a limited time to live. They become present oriented, they get their priorities reordered, they actively get their lives, wishes and desires into high gear and they try to make every minute count.

It is my hope that this book will be of personal assistance to you if you try to assume, from this point on, that you have either just gotten a reprieve from death's door or you have been told that you only have a limited time to live.

Both of these assumptions are inherently true. You know too well how, in a fraction of a second, your life can be snuffed away as one would blow out a flame. Circumstances beyond your control—earthquakes, accidents, etc.—in the blink of an eye can irrevocably alter your life or can terminate it entirely. So assume that you're living on "borrowed time." Commit to not just counting your days but, more importantly, to make every day count, starting with today!

PRESCRIPTION NO. 1

Do it now! Say it now! Enjoy it now!

- Don't assume you will have a tomorrow to reconcile with a loved one, to attend your child's recital, to whisper a word of tenderness, love or encouragement, to take that trip, to make that telephone call, to make amends.

- You are only guaranteed this moment. Make the most of it!

- Embrace a mindset of urgency, curiosity, interest and appreciation for the opportunity to be alive.

- Don't take people, experiences or time for granted. As the song from the play *La Cage Aux Folles* says, "The best of times is now!"

CHAPTER 2

Do You Love Life in the Abstract?

If someone were to ask you, "What do you want out of life?" the answer you most likely would give is, "I want to be happy (whatever that means), healthy, wealthy, have peace of mind," etc. Yet if you were able to be the proverbial fly on the wall and just watch yourself in action, day in and day out, as you prioritize your activities, set your goals, interact with others and make decisions, you might very well scream out in utter disgust, "WHAT AM I DOING?" and "WHAT AM I THINKING?" Perhaps you would recoil in amazement and frustration at the self–defeating attitudes and behaviors you would observe. You might see a total disconnect between what you say you want and the way you go about trying to achieve it.

This paradox is effectively illustrated by the story of The Philosophy Professor. There once was a philosophy professor who was paving his driveway when suddenly some young children came running down the street and ran across the wet cement, leaving a trail of footprints on his driveway. The philosophy professor was livid and incensed by this act. He began chasing and screaming at these children as they ran away. When he returned home, all out of breath, his wife, in utter disbelief at his behavior, said, "How can, you, a philosophy professor, who has always expressed your love for children, explain your hostile behavior towards those children? They obviously did not know the cement was wet." Without a moment's hesitation, the philosophy professor responded, "My dear, I love children in the *abstract* but not in the *concrete*."

This little story represents more than just a play on the words "abstract and concrete." It is indicative of how many of us live our lives. We tend to espouse our love of life, our desire for health, wealth, love and happiness in abstract terms, yet if we observe and analyze some of our day-to-day behaviors, we must begin to question whether we truly are willing to do whatever is required, in the concrete, to realize these goals.

Let's be specific for a moment. If you equate, at least in the abstract, that being a parent will help you to attain personal happiness and fulfillment, then you should ask yourself what does it really require, in concrete, day-to-day, terms to be a great parent? Are you willing to make the sacrifices that will be required of you in terms of time, money, energy, lack of sleep, guidance, curtailed social life? If you say something like, "Well, I want to be a great parent, but I'm not about to give up my social life or quit my job to stay home or work a second job to cover the extra expenses," then you love being a parent in the abstract but not in the concrete. In short, don't have children at this point, because it would be unfair to them.

If you say that you want to get married because you believe that will make you happy and fulfilled, then you have to ask yourself what is involved in being a great husband or wife? Are you willing to share decision making on things over which you now have total control? Are you willing to compromise, not always get your way, do things that at times you don't like to do, be less selfish, be more of a giver than a taker? If you answer "no" to some or all of these questions, then you like being married in the abstract but not in the concrete. Suggestion: Don't get married at this point in your life.

Several years ago, when I first went to work for a major corporation as Director of Organizational Development and Sales Training, I began my career with the goal of eventually becoming a vice president. However, it did not take long for me to observe the other vice presidents, their work schedules, travel schedules and the other responsibilities associated with being a vice president. I am a very family-oriented person, my three children, at that time, were all under the age of ten, and I was honest enough with myself to know that the salary and perks of being a vice president were, for me, not sufficient to make the required sacrifices. So I conscientiously did my job, to the best of my abilities, but I did not do those additional things that would put me on the career path to be a vice president. I was able to objectively say, "I love being a vice president in the abstract, but I am not willing to do those concrete things necessary to be one in the concrete."

Once I made that conscious decision, I never regretted it, never beat myself up for not accomplishing it and never begrudged any of my colleagues who ultimately became vice presidents. The point is to consciously decide what you really want in relation to your values and your willingness to make sacrifices. It is not an issue of right or wrong; rather it's an issue of self-honesty vs. dishonesty. First decide what you really want and why, and then adjust your attitudes and behaviors accordingly.

In fact, too often many of your actions do not promote your goals of health, wealth, love, happiness or whatever you say you'd like to have. As I mentioned, your behaviors frequently are counterproductive and work against your attaining your objectives. The disconnect between your goals and your actions creates in too many of you a high degree of frustration and confusion. You either consciously or subconsciously have not committed to do whatever is necessary to achieve success. Intellectually you have made a commitment, but emotionally and practically you are not willing to make the necessary sacrifices, so whatever you do or don't do only sabotages your dreams and denies you the opportunity to be more satisfied with your life.

Here are a few quick steps to help you clarify and achieve what you really want to achieve:

1. Identify your goal.
2. Ask yourself, "Why is this important to me?"
3. Ask yourself, "How badly do I really want it at this point in my life?"
4. Evaluate how realistic and achievable this goal is at this point in time.
5. Level with yourself as to what sacrifices are required to achieve this goal.

6. Be honest with yourself as to your ability and willingness to pursue this goal.

7. **Decision time: Do it with all your heart or Postpone it or Drop It.**

Whatever your decision, be willing to accept it and be at peace with yourself.

If you are in a "go" mode, then close your eyes for a moment or look in the mirror and try to be totally honest with yourself. You can probably identify some of those potential "toxins" in your own personality that might prevent you from attaining your goal: laziness, immaturity, short attention span; need for immediate gratification; jealousy, egotism, etc. To achieve greater personal and professional satisfaction, all you need do is ask the cooperation and support of the person you see when you close your eyes or look in the mirror. You must be willing to identify the "toxins" and take control of them!

We've all heard the cliché, "We are our own worst enemy." Throughout this book, I show my respect for and belief in the importance of clichés and famous quotes. Despite our tendency as "sophisticated" people to frequently demean and dismiss clichés and quotes as valueless, I suggest that many clichés, if followed, will help lead us to the path of happiness.

For example, William Shakespeare hit the nail on the head when he wrote, "This above all: to thine own self be true." The simplicity and brevity of that statement represents the key to a happier and more fulfilling life for all of us. Yet for a variety of reasons, most of us are not willing or able to insert the key and unlock the door to our inner lives. To be true to yourself, to listen to your inner voice, to truly hear your thoughts, feelings and emotions, to take the time to confront the truth is a difficult and sometimes scary task. In fact, many people take that look and then deny what they see. Sometimes our idealized image of what we would like to be, and what we want others to see in us is not consistent with reality. For instance, ideally we may want to be seen as a helpful, giving, caring individual, but an honest look into our internal mirror may reveal a selfish, manipulative, calculating individual. It takes a very "together" person to not reject what he or she sees in the mirror.

As you take that inner look, keep in mind another saying: "If it ain't broke, don't fix it." That means don't become overly self critical to the point that you try to do a major personality overhaul when all that may be called for is a little "fine tuning." It's like the story of the man who was told by his doctor that he would need an operation. When he informed the doctor that he was in a financial bind and couldn't afford the operation, his doctor replied, "Don't worry, I'll just touch up the X-ray instead." Most of us have a tendency to be too hard on ourselves. Thus, when we get on a self-improvement "kick," we immediately prepare to do major psychosurgery when all that's really needed are some cosmetic repairs. So think of how you can "touch up" your personality X-ray.

PRESCRIPTION NO. 2

Make your decisions based on reality, not fantasy

- Abstractions are great in the world of art, but use concrete, realistic reasoning when making decisions in your personal life.

- Be honest with yourself and others, even if you don't like what you see.

- Determine how badly you want something and what sacrifices you are willing to make to get it. If the clarity and passion are not present, then, for now, pass on it.

- Don't beat yourself up over your decision. Accept it and move on.

CHAPTER 3

Can You Lift a Car?

When people complain that they're "burned out," I suggest to them that they probably were never even "ignited," let alone burned out.

Most of us are underachievers who do not think, work or develop to our true potential. Although scientists are still wrestling with identifying the limits of our physical and mental abilities, there is already a definite consensus among psychologists, psychiatrists, behaviorists and researchers that most of us are operating way below our capabilities.

The complexity and power of the human mind are awesome. Periodically, through studies or under unusual circumstances or periods of extreme crisis, examples surface of how an individual's mind or body can perform in an extraordinary fashion. Documented cases of men and women of average or below average size and strength lifting an automobile off a pinned-down person, child prodigies who solve complicated mathematical equations and the like all attest to the untapped capability of the human mind and body and spirit.

So if these things can be done, why don't more of us perform them more frequently? One possible answer is that too many of us intentionally set and accept low standards and lim-

its of personal performance. Why run the risk of disappointment? Let's compare your life to a bar being set for a high
jumper. If you set the bar only to the height over which you
are sure you can jump, then time and again you can make the
jump successfully. It's human nature not to want to experience the feelings that come with failure. Many of us have grown
up being taught that success is to be attained and failure is to
be avoided.

However, the fallacy of such reasoning is that you often
cannot experience great success without first experiencing
failure. The two concepts are interrelated. Therefore, in all areas of your life, it's important that you constantly raise the bar,
thereby increasing your risk of failure while at the same time
increasing your chances for new successes. To really live, you
must constantly try to hurdle over greater and more demanding challenges. If in fact you reach a plateau beyond which
you cannot seem to go or beyond which you do not choose to
go, then stay in shape so that you can repeatedly stay at that
level of performance.

Life must be challenging to be fulfilling. However, be sure
to set your own bar at a height *you* desire to overcome, and
don't let others set the height for you. Remember, in the high
jump, the athlete's objective is primarily to compete against
her own best jump, to compete against herself. A jumper may
take pride in achieving her own best performance even if she
does not win the competition against other jumpers.

So too in life you might often concentrate on "beating out" others rather than striving for your own best performance. Concentrating your energies on competing with others can lead to anxiety, frustration, antagonism and self-doubt. Why not leave the making of those comparisons to others? Take the pressure off yourself and channel your energies into doing the very best you can. After all, whether you want it or not, others are constantly making comparative judgments about you anyway. You're being compared with others in almost every area of your life. Who will make a better dating partner, spouse, employee, friend? The point here is to make your presentation and performance hinge more on your own desire to do and be the best you can rather than on your desire to top the competition. You can experience the pride and satisfaction of being a "winner" if you make that judgment based upon your own best efforts.

When I gave the analogy of the high jumper setting her own height for the bar sufficiently high to cause her to extend her abilities to the fullest, it reminded me of the classic story of the 85-year-old man who was engaged to a 20-year-old woman. The old man goes to his doctor for his premarital blood test. The doctor, aware of the great difference in age between the bride and groom, is greatly concerned about how the old man's heart will withstand the strain of the honeymoon night. Finally, the doctor looks at the 85-year-old man and says, "You know, this marriage could prove fatal," to which the old man replies, "Look, if she dies, she dies." What confidence!

In life, if you are going to make it in whatever you do, you must have confidence in yourself. You must believe that you can and will accomplish your objectives. However, many of you, over the course of your life, may have had your confidence in yourself eroded through the programming of others, who have told you that "you can't," "you shouldn't," "you did a bad job," etc. You may have actually begun to doubt your abilities.

Why don't you take a lesson from the bumblebee? Did you know that according to the laws of aerodynamics the bumblebee should not be able to fly? The relation of its wingspan to its body weight is such that the bumblebee should be unable to get off the ground. But nobody has told the bumblebee, so that sucker keeps buzzing around and fertilizing the flowers. Shouldn't someone inform Mr. Bumblebee that he is not supposed to be able to fly so that he'll get back on the ground where he belongs?

Many of us have been told by well-intentioned parents, friends, family members and teachers, "Hey, you can't fly!" Well, they didn't exactly use those words; the message was more specific. We were told such things as, "You can't sing," "You can't draw," "You aren't good in math," "You don't speak foreign languages well," "You'll never amount to anything," "You'll always be poor." These negative "you can't" messages were delivered, received and perhaps accepted by you as truth. Unlike the bumblebee, who is smart enough not to listen to people who tell him he can't fly, some of you have in fact stayed grounded and have avoided flapping your physical, emotional, and intellectual wings because someone told you that you couldn't.

Let me urge you to look at those areas of your life where you lack confidence or which have gone unexplored, and let me suggest that you try to get off the ground and do some flying. If nothing else, at least flap your wings and see how it feels. I believe that people were placed on this earth to fly as high and as far as possible. You owe it to yourself to try.

A supposedly true story dramatically illustrates how we underestimate our own abilities. Several years ago, in a graduate course of higher mathematics, a college student arrived late to class for his final examination. When he arrived, the exam was already in progress, and the professor handed the student a sheet of paper with some math problems. The student also noticed three additional math problems on the front blackboard. Having come late, the student completed the problems on the paper, but did not have time to begin the problems on the blackboard. He asked the professor if he could work on those problems back in his dormitory and turn them in the next day. The professor agreed. He turned them in, having only completed one of the three problems.

The following day, the professor showed up at the student's room yelling, "You did it! You did it!" in reaction to which the student almost apologetically responded, "Why, no, Professor,

I only completed one of those three problems." The professor explained, "You came late to the exam, and you didn't hear me when I gave the instructions to the class. I told them, 'Here on this sheet of paper is your final exam. In addition, I'm placing on the blackboard three problems that even Albert Einstein could not solve.' And you solved one of them!"

This story dramatizes a significant point. If you, or most of the people you know, had been in that class, if you had arrived for your exam on time, if you had heard the professor say, "And on the blackboard are three problems that even Albert Einstein couldn't solve," you probably would have reacted, "If Einstein couldn't solve them, then I sure as heck can't."

Human nature is such that most of us would never even have attempted the problems, let alone solved one. However, the student in the story never heard that programming. He assumed that he was not only *expected* to solve the problems but that he also had the *ability* to solve them. Having that positive mindset, lo and behold, he actually solved one of those problems. The two critical concepts that influence what you will get out of your life are the "expectations" you set for yourself and others and the "abilities" you ascribe to yourself and others. They consciously and subconsciously influence behavior and results.

Who knows what your limits are? No doubt there are limits to your physical and mental abilities, but why not keep stretching and challenging yourself to find out how far you can go? If you've ever participated in a calisthenics program, then you have probably experienced a situation where you're doing pushups, and your body is aching and screaming at you with every muscle, "Stop, I can't do any more," while at the same time, the exercise instructor is screaming at you to "do one more!" Had you been in the room by yourself, you probably would have stopped, but you found that with the urging of the instructor you could, in fact, do one or more additional pushups.

That's what life is all about. No matter what you do, you should constantly push yourself to "do one more." Most of the time you'll find that you had more energy, ability, and desire left inside you than you thought you had. And don't limit yourself to pushing your mental performance. Of equal or even greater importance is stretching your emotional performance. You can love more, care more, share more, smile more, listen more, reinforce others more, and the list goes on.

I am a big fan of the late and great singer, Al Jolson. Whether you're too young to remember him or not, please consider one of his signature remarks that he would share with his audience when performing. Upon completion of a song that had brought the audience to tears or cheers, he would say, "Folks, you ain't seen nothin' yet!" Why don't you adapt that philosophy and keep raising your bar?

PRESCRIPTION NO. 3

Set high goals and force yourself to stretch

- Don't underestimate your abilities or those of others.

- No matter how hard you try and how much you achieve, you can still try harder and go farther if you **stretch**.

- Remember the saying, "If you reach for the sky, you won't end up with a handful of mud."

CHAPTER 4

There But for the Grace of God

Question—in terms of demonstrating a drive, a desire and a willingness to act so as to attain self-fulfillment, is the concept of "motivation" a **luxury** or a **necessity** of life? This is an important question, because the answer has definite implications for how you approach the issue of motivation in your own life.

Let's lay the groundwork for answering this question by my suggesting that initially we take a global view of people and of life. The people on this great planet Earth can be categorized and divided into many groupings. However, for our purpose of considering the luxury vs. necessity aspects of motivation, let's classify Earth's population into three broad categories.

Category I is a very large population of people who live primarily in underdeveloped countries under extreme conditions of abject poverty. These are the people who are literally starving and dying by the hour. The television newscasts have opened the eyes and hearts of the world to the pitiful sight of physically emaciated children and parents in Darfur, for example. A combination of famine, disease, inadequate shelter and climatic disasters of drought, monsoons, hurricanes, earthquakes, coupled with political and racial genocide have decimated or destroyed hundreds of thousands of our fellow human beings. The day-to-day existence of those who still cling to life involves a desperate fight for survival, and their lives are filled with despair, pain, suffering, helplessness and torment.

People who live under such wretched conditions are pre-occupied not with thriving but rather with surviving. Abraham Maslow's Hierarchy of Needs suggests that until people are, to some acceptable level, able to meet their basic needs for food, water, clothing, shelter, self-esteem and love, they are not in a position to pursue their higher needs of ego gratification, self-fulfillment and self-actualization. His concept is often shown as a pyramid:

Actualization (meaning self-fulfillment)

↑

Esteem (includes self-esteem)

↑

Love/Belonging

↑

Safety [includes shelter]

↑

Physiological (including food and water)

People who live in abject poverty do not listen to motivational tapes, do not attend motivational lectures nor buy motivational books. For them, motivation is an issue of basic survival and necessity. Striving for greater self-fulfillment would be an absurd luxury.

The Category II segment of the world's population are those fellow human beings who live under totalitarian regimes in such places as Cuba, Iran, Beijing or North Korea. Whereas motivational programs available in free-world societies encourage individual creativity, limitless opportunity, self-expression, risk-taking and the right and obligation to pursue self-fulfillment, the citizens of these totalitarian systems are taught conformity, compliance to authority and limitations on self-expression. The emphasis is on "Thou Shall Not," "Thou Will Not" and "Thou Cannot." Were I to, or any other motivational speaker, attempt to speak in any of these countries or try to make available any of our books or tapes, we would quickly find ourselves arrested and our materials confiscated. We would be viewed and treated as "enemies of the state."

However, millions of these people do not need the external stimulation of a motivator to know that they want more out of life than they are allowed to have in their current repressive environment. They are so hungry and so desperate for the opportunity to be free that they literally risk their lives to try to escape to the free world. Just think of the commitment and level of motivation and desire one must have to be willing to risk one's life, expose oneself to injury and risk prison, loss of family, friends, cultural roots and all possessions—all for the promise of freedom. These people believe in the words of the Statue of Liberty: "Give me your tired, your poor, your huddled masses yearning to be free." **Such people view motivation as a necessity of life, not a luxury.** They are willing to endure, struggle and take risks that will place them in an environment where striving for self-fulfillment is even possible.

Have you even noticed how many immigrants approach life once they do escape from totalitarian societies? Although I'm generalizing, they tend to be so motivated to achieve their personal and professional dreams that they are willing to do just about anything and make whatever sacrifices are necessary to be successful. It if means working two or three jobs, going to school to learn English, a trade, a profession; or skimping, saving and postponing short-term gratification for long-term gratification, or risk-taking, investing, etc., they are willing to do so. Having lived for years where they were denied these opportunities and having sacrificed to escape, they are totally committed to realize their dreams and aspirations.

Category III is the segment of the Earth's population of which you and I are a part. You live neither in abject poverty nor under a totalitarian government. You do not worry about basic survival; in fact, you are probably more concerned with dieting and losing weight than you are about an empty, hungry stomach. No government prohibits you in any way from pursuing your dreams and aspirations; in fact, you are encouraged to do so. Free-world governments are predicated and dependent for their success on the expectation that citizens will be ambitious, creative and motivated enough to develop new processes, technologies, jobs, and goods and services that will enhance the economic and social quality of life. Therefore the environment is in place for supporting the pursuit of your personal and professional dreams.

Yet many of you reading this book may take for granted your good fortune. Whether by accident of birth or, if you believe, through some preconceived plan, the fact remains that many of you were born free rather than in a country like Ethiopia or North Korea. No matter how rough you believe your life has been, it's doubtful that you would voluntarily choose to trade places with either of the other two categories of populations discussed.

So what's the point of discussing the "have-nots" and "cannots" of the world? It is to perhaps **shake you out of your complacency**. You can go through the motions of reading motivational books, listening to motivational tapes and attending motivational lectures from now to the end of your life. However, if you don't act and begin to apply what you hear, read and observe into concrete action that can improve your life, then you are depriving yourself of a precious gift and opportunity that others would desperately love to have.

If you don't take advantage of your good fortune, of the

fact that you are part of that minority of people on this planet who can thrive and not merely survive, then in my opinion, it's akin to your committing a sin.

Don't waste the chance to dream dreams. Don't waste the precious opportunity to make those dreams come true! There are millions of people who would risk everything they have, including their lives, to trade places with you. **You may not be able to help them, but you sure as heck can help yourself!** Stop taking so many priceless things in your life for granted. Use every day, every hour, every minute to promote your happiness and the happiness of others. Start living every day as if you were an immigrant to this country, who just escaped abject poverty or a repressive regime. Try to think, feel and act with the same appreciation and zest to be here and with the same hunger to succeed that they would exhibit.

Dr. Fred's

PRESCRIPTION NO. 4

Think and act like a motivated immigrant

- You are a member of the lucky minority on this planet.

- You really have few excuses to fall back on.

- Don't squander your good fortune. "Go for the gold."

- To realize your dreams and aspirations, think, act and sacrifice as if you were an immigrant to this country.

CHAPTER 5

Squeeze Your Orange of Life!

If you can visualize your life as a big, ripe, juicy orange waiting to be squeezed, then you can begin to understand why some people's cup of life is full of juice while other people's cups are pretty empty. The difference depends upon the fervor with which you squeeze the orange. Those who have a very full cup are really thirsty, so they take that big ol' orange and bring all their energy and strength to bear as they squeeze every last drop of juice out of it. Even when it looks as if the orange is bone dry, they take one extra hard squeeze and then suck out the remaining pulp for good measure.

Those people who have less than full cups seem not to be all that thirsty or they must not have the strength and or the desire to get life's juices. They rather politely and tentatively approach their "Orange of Life," and then they gently squeeze or "tweak" it so that a few drops trickle out. For as long as possible, they savor those few drops because they have no plans nor reason to expect any more juice will be forthcoming.

How thirsty are you for life's many good things? How strongly can you taste the sweetness of health, wealth, love, joy, contentment and the other juices of life? Does the thought of those juices make you salivate with desire and commitment for their attainment? Do you want to drink so badly that you're willing to exert all the physical, mental and emotional energy necessary to "squeeze the orange"? You must ask yourself these questions if you wish to improve the quality of your life.

Perhaps the entire discussion can be reduced to one word: "passion." Webster defines "passion" as intense emotion, compelling action. Usually we think of passion in the context of a love relationship between two people, but it is equally logical to apply the yardstick of passion to measure how much you are in love with life. That same burning, fervent desire should be present and evident in your attitude toward your life, and you should live passionately every day.

Unless you are emotionally disturbed, you probably don't want to die. If someone or something were to threaten your life, you would do everything in your power to preserve it. You would forfeit your most precious personal possessions, you might physically fight for your life, you might beg or even commit an illegal act if that were the only way to save yourself. In essence, you would demonstrate that you passionately didn't want to die. But to passionately not want to die is not the same thing as saying that you passionately want to live. In one instance, you want to preserve your life processes and the status quo that represents your existence on earth. You desperately want to avoid death.

However, to want to **live** your life with a passion is to desire to get everything possible that life has to offer you. The issue then becomes one of thriving rather than merely want-ing to survive. Each minute you are still breathing, each inter-action you have with another person, each experience you have to learn and participate is another opportunity to squeeze your orange. Remember to cherish these opportunities and to take advantage of your good fortune to do so. You want to mini-mize the regrets you will have at the end of your journey. It is imperative that you maintain an attitude of passion and a sense of urgency as you squeeze your "Orange of Life." Although passion and all emotions should be tempered by a degree of reason, avoid being so cerebral and rational that you lose the drive and momentum necessary to achieve your goals.

Time is such an unpredictable variable in our lives that we cannot assume its indefinite availability; thus we must com-bine a sense of urgency with our passion and enthusiasm. Resist the temptation to postpone action on your goals and dreams. Try to develop an attitude that says, "I must do it now or at least get started." For many of you, being passionate to-ward your life and feeling a sense of urgency is a new and perhaps totally foreign notion. You may have always operated as a "mañana" (put it off till tomorrow) person. You may won-der whether you really can or in fact should shift into high gear.

The answer to that concern is simple: You're under no obligation, nor should you feel guilty or dissatisfied if you choose not to live your life at the speed of light. The choice should and must be yours. Each reader will decide to what degree, if at all, to adopt and practice the ideas discussed in this book. However, you should recognize that a cause-and-effect relationship does exist between the attitude with which you approach your life and the satisfaction that you will experience. So gently squeeze your orange if your goals are modest, but then be content with what you get. However, if you have not as yet satisfied your goals and desires and if you still want to achieve them, then get serious, roll up your sleeves, become more passionate, become more conscious of time and start squeezing that orange till your thirst is quenched. It will give you your needed dosage of Vitamin C—for Contentment.

PRESCRIPTION NO. 5

Squeeze your "orange of life" with all your might!

- Think of your life as a big orange waiting to be squeezed.

- The amount of time, energy and effort you expend in squeezing will determine the amount of "juice" in your cup.

- Make sure your hand aches so your cup will "runneth over."

CHAPTER 6

Stop the Treadmill!

It is probably not unusual for you to find yourself so consumed and caught up in the hectic flow of day-to-day living that one day quickly melts into the next, with little or no time taken to evaluate where you've been or where you are going. The days quickly become weeks, the weeks become months, and the months, years. Life becomes a series of fragmented activities that often bear no relation to your aspirations and expectations of life.

One way to prevent such an aimless, dissatisfying approach to your life is to periodically call a "Time Out." This involves a physical, mental and emotional withdrawal from the routines of life that allows you to sit down and evaluate what is happening and what you feel should be happening in your life. Such a conscious period for reflection and assessment can provide you with opportunities for making course corrections where needed.

Running on the "Treadmill of Life" can be exhilarating and satisfying, or it can be draining, boring and frustrating. Do you ever get caught in the trap of trying to stay on the treadmill and trying to keep pace? Do you find yourself running for the roses without taking time out to smell them?

Sometimes the pace can become so frantic and frenetic that you can lose sight of your goals and your purpose for staying on the treadmill. Often your goals can become diluted and reduced to short-range maintenance activities, such as, "If I can only make it to the weekend, I'll be okay," "If I can only make it to my vacation, I'll be okay," and finally the ultimate objective, "If I can only make it to my retirement, then I'll be okay."

In each instance, running on the "Treadmill of Life" takes on a momentum of its own. This momentum often becomes more rooted in your instincts for survival than in fulfilling your deepest desire for personal and professional fulfillment. If you're not careful, a mindset of thriving and aspiring may be replaced by a mindset of mediocrity, coping, making it and getting by,

It's not unusual for you perhaps to yearn to either temporarily or permanently get off your treadmill. In some instances, you may wish to remain on, but also to slow down the pace. Or perhaps you wish to get on a different treadmill altogether, one that faces toward a different direction. Only you can make that personal decision. However, you are really shortchanging yourself if you don't periodically evaluate where you're going. The truth is that it is often much easier and emotionally safer to keep yourself moving on the "Treadmill of Life" than it is to temporarily shut off the current so that you can rest and ponder the questions, "Where am I going?" "Why do

I want to go there?", "Is there another way to get where I want to go?", "Why am I doing what I'm doing?", "Is there some-place else I would rather go or should be going to?"

I urge you to ask yourself these questions. The current path you have chosen may feel safe and comfortable to you, but it may not necessarily be in your long-term best interest. This is another exercise in going out of your comfort zone: Stop your treadmill long enough to evaluate and ponder these questions and then be able to say, "Yes, to my own self, I have been true."

PRESCRIPTION NO. 6

Define what you want out of life

- In the book *Alice in Wonderland* is the famous line, "If you don't know where you are going, then any road will get you there."

- Periodically, call time out from your treadmill.

- Review, revisit, re-evaluate your values and goals before getting back on.

CHAPTER 7

Keep 'em Spinning

You have probably seen this act on a television variety show or perhaps at a carnival or circus. A performer, usually a man dressed in black pants with an open-necked shirt, accompanied by an assistant, comes on stage to the pulsating background music of the "Flight of the Bumble Bee" or some other frenetic tempo. His assistant has a stack of dinner plates in her hand, and the stage is set with a series of five to eight long sticks set on a table. The performer begins by spinning one or two plates atop each stick, then adds a third, runs back to increase the spin of the first two plates, adds a fourth and fifth plate, runs back to spin the first three, and on and on.

The more plates the performer attempts to spin, the more frantic becomes his pace of running among the plates trying to keep them all spinning. At that moment, his greatness nightmare is that one or more plates will come crashing to the ground. Thankfully for him, his act lasts only two to four minutes, and then the music mercifully indicates that his performance is over. His assistant grabs the plates off the sticks, he gives a dramatic bow and the audience offers him a resounding round of applause as he dashes off the stage.

As you visualize that act in your mind, do you see an analogy with how you at times live your life? Either by choice or necessity, do you undertake and accept many responsibilities that are akin to the plates in this illustration? If so, you probably don't bring just a few plates to the "Stage of Life"; you in fact bring *stacks* of "dishes." You have a "Family Stack" composed of individual plates, each representing a member of your family. You perhaps have a plate for your spouse and each of your children, a plate for your mother, your father, your sister, your brother, Uncle Louie, etc. You also have a "Job Stack" of dishes composed of individual plates that represent each of your job responsibilities. You can also have several additional stacks of dishes: "Chore Stack," "Social Stack," "Community/ Volunteer Stack," "Spiritual Stack," "Relaxation/Fun Stack," and the list goes on.

Understandably, you feel that each plate is important and must be kept "spinning." Thus you run from activity to activity trying to keep all your plates spinning and desperately trying to prevent any one of them from crashing down around you. As you get older and as your involvements increase and your life becomes more complex, you may feel that you are responsible for spinning more plates than you can handle. The more things you undertake, the harder you run. Without thinking, you may tend to treat all your "plates" and all your "stacks" with the same level of importance. You are petrified of being perceived or accused of neglecting any of your plates. You are totally committed to ensuring that none of your plates fall or go unattended. Over time, you begin to feel more acutely both the physical and emotional stress and strain of performing this act. In short, you are exhausted!

What, if anything, could or should you do when confronted with this situation? The first thing to remember is that *you* must take primary responsibility for deciding how to respond. However, if you keep our illustration in mind, you will probably agree that there are physical limits as to how many plates you can realistically spin at any one time, and there are limits as to which stacks can and should receive your attention. The truth is that at different stages of your life, different plates and stacks deserve your attention or need to be kept "spinning." It's an issue of degree, frequency and priorities. It is not an all or nothing situation.

If you are a student, then it should be your education stack and its plates that deserve and need your spinning. If you are a newlywed, then it should be your spouse and marriage that needs to be spun. If you have young children, then it should be them that you keep spinning. If you are building a career, then it should be your job that you keep spinning. If you are retired, then it should be the things you always wanted to have time to do that should get your primary spin time.

I acknowledge that I am making a generalization here, but I believe more women than men must struggle with the spinning plates phenomenon. Women who try to juggle career, domestic and child-rearing responsibilities often become emotional and physical victims of trying to accommodate too many plates in their lives. This reality is effectively illustrated by the comment made by late and great Ginger Rogers regarding her responsibilities as compared to Fred Astaire, her dance partner. She said (and I paraphrase), "I do the same thing as Fred Astaire, only I have to do it wearing heels and moving backwards." Many women today are spinning plates just like their male counterparts, only they often are spinning more plates and often at a more hectic pace

Now, at any given time, you should be prepared to receive some flak from the people whose plates are not being spun. They may complain that they are being ignored. If you are a newlywed, you might hear that complaint from your parents: "We hardly see you anymore. Don't you love us?" Some people may try to make you feel guilty. At your job, supervisors may try a "guilt trip" to get you to stay late or work extra hours on the weekend when you may prefer to be at home with your family. Friends may tease you, claiming that you no longer care about them.

You must be prepared for such flak and be strong enough not to cave in to these verbal and emotional assaults. You need to be in charge of deciding which of your "plates" are most important to you at any given time and which warrant your energy and time to spin. You must also take responsibility for determining the number of plates you can handle effectively and with comfort. This latter consideration of your limits is something that can be best determined through a trial-and-error process. If you are willing and sensitive enough to tune into your mind and body, then they will let you know if and when you're overloading your circuits.

When your internal warning light signals "overload," you must then be ready and willing, either permanently or temporarily, to let something go. If you refuse to listen to and acknowledge the warning signs, then over time you can expect to have the decision taken out of your hands and made for you by the circumstances you have created.

Even the most disciplined and well-managed workaholic will ultimately face the consequences of her unwillingness or inability to understand and accept the "Law of the Spinning Plates." Now, the consequences can take many forms and have varying degrees of effect. For example, on one end of the continuum of consequences might be increased inefficiency and ineffectiveness in the quality of how you handle your various commitments and responsibilities. On the other extreme end of the continuum might be your death, a death caused by the cumulative effect of physiological and psychological conditions that you allowed to develop and fester over years of self-abuse and neglect. In between these extremes lie a host of other consequences, including marital and other relationships that deteriorate, hypertension, and the list goes on.

You have to ask yourself: How much is enough and how much is too much? When does the law of diminishing returns take effect? When are you putting more into a situation than you're taking out? You must answer the age-old question, "Is it better to do a few things well, or a lot of things poorly?" For most of us, the answer is neither black nor white, but resides in a gray area. It is also true that each of us varies in our abilities, flexibilities, energy level, and organizational and time management skills. These differences help explain why some of us are better than others in the number of plates we are able to spin. If you wish to effectively take on more plates, then you must improve in some of these areas.

Unlike our abstractly discussing issues of effective living in a book or conversation, the answers in real life are not pure, nor clear cut. You must be conscious of what's going on in your life, and then try to make some adjustments and do the best you can. Just try not to replicate the act of the performer who was trying to spin more plates than was humanly possible. He ended up running off the stage, and so might you!

PRESCRIPTION NO. 7

Each day, spin only your priority "plates"

- The "Law of the Spinning Plates" is grounded in common sense.

- Accept the physical, emotional and time limitations you have on how many "plates" you can realistically spin at any one time.

- Each day, decide to focus your energies and time on your priority plates and spin the others when you can.

- The life you save may be your own!

CHAPTER 8

Beware of the Minefields

Life is like a minefield. What a vivid mental image that conjures up! Strewn across the field of your life, as you move forward minute to minute, hour to hour, day to day and year to year are hidden, unexpected problems, crises and catastrophes that periodically blow up in your face.

Have you ever felt as if you were trying to navigate your way across your personal minefield of life? Each decision you have to make may lead you to a safe area or to an emotional explosion. Sometimes such a view of life may result in an overly cautious approach to decision making because of your preoccupation with avoiding the "mines." If this is the case, then you may find that your indecision can become a danger that causes you more harm than the perceived mine. After all, to not make a decision is in fact a decision that still has consequences. If this is your view and experience in your life, what can be done? You must bring in your "minesweepers" to detect where the mines in your life have been planted, and then begin the process of defusing and removing them.

You ask, "That sounds great, but what exactly are my minesweepers?" Minesweepers can take several forms and combinations, such as past experience, logical reasoning, intuition, objective observation, effective listening skills, external advice or professional counseling. Although you cannot detect and/or diffuse all the mines, you *can* begin clearing a wide enough safety path to permit you to pursue a course of action that offers you a greater degree of confidence and optimism for success.

Let's reduce this to a concrete example. You have been dating a guy or gal regularly for six months and are beginning to wonder whether to take that fateful step to the altar. You begin fantasizing what it would be like to be married to this person. Your heart and your mind become embroiled in a heated debate. Your heart argues that the warm, secure, good feelings you experience when you're together surely are sufficient reasons to decide in favor of marriage.

However, your brain creates nagging, uncomfortable feelings of doubt as it reminds you how different are your personalities, values, family backgrounds, religions and temperaments. "Remember," says your brain, "how often you two argue over basic issues and how you're always made to give in even when you feel that you're right." Well, this little debate can rage forever as you try to decide whether or not he is the person with whom you really should share the rest of your life.

In an effort to avoid the mines of unhappiness that are planted on the "marital minefield," you suddenly become immobilized as to whether to pursue or drop the relationship.

Suddenly your whole life becomes affected, and your job performance, appetite, sleep pattern and other relationships suffer as you agonize over this decision. How can you sweep the minefields? The first minesweeping tool that you could use is to write down, in priority order, those criteria for mate selection that are important to you. For a moment, forget about the specific person you're considering. Instead, think of criteria you would apply to any potential mate and write them down. Then as objectively as possible, begin to evaluate this person in relation to those criteria.

Next, ask your boyfriend to go through the same process of evaluating you in relation to his criteria. Then sit down and discuss, together, the results of your evaluations. Try to determine, together, the potential pitfalls of such a marriage and evaluate the degree of impact they might have on your mutual happiness. It might also be wise to go for premarital counseling to discuss with a professional the assets and liabilities each of you would bring into the relationship. Finally, resort to the least scientific but very reliable process of listening to your heart and your intuition. When you listen to your heart, listen for the honest message that it's sending, even if it's not what you really want to hear.

Any or all of these procedures will sweep the mines from a potentially unhappy marriage. This process can increase the likelihood of knowing where the remaining mines are buried and will offer both of you insights into how to walk around them or defuse them. You may also come to the conclusion that there are too many mines to contend with and that therefore you should not pursue the relationship.

Many of the mines you encounter in your personal and professional life fall into several categories: your own or other's "psychological mines" that consist of irrational fears and anxieties or insecurities and needs that reflect your personality and values; "family mines" that reflect the internal dynamics of those relationships; and "environmental, economic, health or logistical mines" that are beyond your control. Some mines are fairly obvious because they are near the surface and visible. If you have your mind, eyes and ears open, you can't miss them. Other mines are more deeply buried or are camouflaged and will require that you actively be more vigilant and deliberate with your caution, intuition and objectivity if you are to detect them before it's too late. They are like icebergs that can deliver significant damage if not identified before impact. In any event, you must keep moving forward. You cannot allow yourself to be immobilized, discouraged or frightened away from pursuing your goals as you search for happiness. The mines will always be before you. You will even occasionally step on one and be injured, but that is the price you must willingly pay for the opportunity to seek happiness and success. Your injury may be minor or severe, but it is very seldom life threatening. You can and will recover, and you must return to the minefields of life—the sooner the better!

When making decisions, use your "minesweepers"

- Experience, intuition and self-awareness are some of the "minesweepers" that will minimize the number of times that you step on one of life's mines. Listen to those minesweepers even if you don't like what they are saying.

- Stepping on a mine from time to time is normal and inevitable but is seldom fatal.

- Learn from the experience.

- Keep moving forward, and don't let fear of life's mines immobilize you.

71

CHAPTER 9

The Lady or the Tiger?

In the classic story, "The Lady or the Tiger?", a young man is placed before two closed doors. Behind one of them is a vicious tiger that will surely devour him, and behind the other is the beautiful maiden he deeply loves. Our hero must make a life-and-death decision. Should he choose the wrong door, the risks, are tremendous. Should he select the right door, the rewards promise fulfillment of his greatest desires. Which door should he choose?

Life in many ways is akin to that story. We are constantly confronted with decisions and choices that offer satisfaction or disappointment, hope or despair, ecstasy or disaster. The consequences of these decisions vary in their degree of impact. Sometimes, regardless of your decision, you can't really lose and sometimes you can't really win. But on occasion, you are confronted with significant decisions with major long-term consequences. Sometimes you can avoid creating situations that necessitate choices. Depending on your age and memory, you may recall that there was once a popular TV show called *Let's Make a Deal*, hosted by Monte Hall. Recently the concept has been revised with a new TV show called *Deal or No Deal*, hosted by Howie Mandel. Both of these shows are really microcosms of life.

In *Let's Make a Deal*, contestants dressed in outrageous-looking costumes sat in the audience, hoping to attract Monte's attention so that they would be selected to come on stage and "make a deal." He would offer them choices of selecting a box or a curtain or money. They could gamble what they won for the unknown possibility of upgrading to a bigger and better prize. Should the contestant take what was in the box, or trade for what was behind one of the curtains, or trade what she had already won for the unknown possibility of a bigger and better prize? When the choices were made and the prizes revealed, did the contestant get a "Clunk" or a "Zap" or did she win the grand prize?

Yes, we are all members of the audience in life's game show called *Let's Make a Deal* or *Deal or No Deal*. We each come to the show hoping to be big winners. We yell and scream, figuratively, "I WANT TO WIN! I WANT TO WIN!" Yet few of us are willing to come out of the audience, get in front of the cameras and actually play under the pressures and risks involved. You see, many people want an iron-clad guarantee, before they take the risks, that they will **definitely, unequivocally, without a doubt, make the right choice and therefore be a winner.**

Since, with few exceptions, such guarantees cannot be given, many of us decide to remain in the audience and seldom, if ever, volunteer to get on stage. We basically live our lives in the "safety zone," which is an imaginary box with definite boundaries within which we live and make decisions regarding our lives. Each person's safety zone varies in size. Some people have created for themselves a safety zone box that is small and narrow, and others have created one that is wide. However, regardless of the size of your safety zone, the common characteristic of all the zone boxes is that they provide comfort and security.

As long as you stay within the parameters of your box, you can at least minimize the risks and possible negative consequence of your decisions. Within the safety zone, you usually know in advance the rules, payoffs and results of your actions. If, however, you were to venture beyond the boundaries of your safety zone, into unknown territory, then you will increase both your chance of success as well as your chances of failure. It can be scary crossing into the "risk zone," but *the risk zone is where the action and fun of life can be found.* It is full of brass rings, phenomenal wealth, prestige, love, happiness and success, as well as minefields and pits of quicksand.

There are usually elements of gambling regardless of whether you live in the safety zone or the risk zone. In the risk zone, the odds are with the house, not with you, the player. But the stakes, payoff, and losses are greater when you win or lose. You, the player, can do some things relative to planning and implementation that can decrease the odds of losing. However, in the final analysis, if you choose to play the game of life with occasional abandon, then you will provide yourself with the opportunity to be a big winner.

Clearly I am neither advocating nor discouraging you from living your life predominantly in the risk zone. You must use some discretion and evaluate what you can afford to risk, what's worth the risk, the timing, and the like. Some of you are more attracted to the risk zone than others. It really becomes a matter of degree. However, *periodic risk taking should be a part of your life.*

You have dreams and aspirations of what you would like to accomplish in your life. Frequently, these dreams are either personal and/or professional in nature. As a rule, they cannot be realized as long as you live entirely in your safety zone. Rather than follow the typical regret pattern of living, which consists of looking back and saying, "If I only had my life to live over again I would _____", it is preferable to load up with ammunition and supplies, clearly identify your objective, select an appropriate path and go on an occasional safari into the risk zone.

Keep in mind two famous sayings: "Most people aim at nothing in life and hit it with amazing accuracy" and "The turtle only makes progress when it sticks its neck out." *Have a goal and be willing to take some risks to achieve it!*

Take risks as often as you can

- The greatest risk in life is not taking a risk. You will never know what you could have had or experienced.

- Take more risks and experience the exhilaration of really feeling alive. It beats the boredom of security and predictability.

- So what if you make a mistake? Most situations are reversible.

- Remember the saying, "You can't get to second base until you take your foot off of first base."

CHAPTER 10

Life is a Garage Sale

Have you ever held a garage sale? If so, you know what it's like to pull together all your "junk," which someone else will see as "riches." For pricing and sale, you must now reappraise and revalue clothes, toys, appliances, furniture and a vast array of items that had a different value when new. In most instances, the items will sell for less than the original purchase price, but in some instances, items will have increased in value from what you paid for them when new. Usually all items are priced for the garage sale at a value higher than what the sellers and buyers feel they are worth. Thus part of the fun in garage sales is the process of negotiation or, to be more direct, bargaining.

My wife and I once had a garage sale. In preparation, we spent many hours rummaging through closets and drawers for items. Before we realized it, we had cartons of items, particularly clothing. The big day arrived, and on a Saturday morning, no sooner had we posted the first "GARAGE SALE" sign than we were invaded by hoards of bargain seekers. Frequently we were offered less for an item than what it was marked. Since it was still morning, we tried to hold out for our price or an offer closer to our price. Suddenly at two o'clock the sky opened up with a heavy downpour. We scrambled to clear the tables of clothes, but we could not compete with the speed of the rain. Our "for sale" clothes were soaking wet. We had to literally wring them out. My wife and I were drenched and looked like proverbial drowned rats. Suddenly the value of these items was dramatically and irrevocably decreased, though they were not totally worthless; perhaps after drying them out, they could be donated as a tax deduction.

We learned a valuable lesson that day: how quickly, through unanticipated events, the value of things can be dramatically changed! Happily this was just a garage sale. The consequences to us of the rainstorm were really minimal. In fact, we were able to laugh at the spectacle of our running around trying to salvage our drenched clothes.

However, in the larger context of life, how often do we undervalue or take for granted our relationships, our possessions or even ourselves? How often do we not truly recognize and appreciate the value of our lives, our family, our friends, and our health until some unexpected rainstorm dilutes, diminishes or destroys them? When this happens we are suddenly jolted into a new reality: that perhaps through complacency, we never quite fully understood and appreciated the value of these things.

There is no question that a downpour of illness, economic hard times, marital difficulties, stress, etc., can wreak havoc with your "pricing system." Relationships that were taken for granted can suddenly become priceless; activities like being able to walk outside your house can take on a whole new value if illness renders you bedridden.

Take a lesson from the garage sale story. Refocus your priorities, sensitivities and feelings. Get back in touch with what is really important to you and that gives meaning to your life. Have you unintentionally mismarked and devalued the people, relationships and other aspects of your life? Have you begun to worship at the altar of materialism? Have you rationalized and justified your neglect of spouse, children, health and self to a "greater good," the acquisition of material security? How big a house, car, wardrobe or jewelry box do you need? How much is enough, and when is it too much?

There is a price tag on almost everything you do. You pay a price not in dollars but rather in time and relationships. Whether you realize it or not, you are having a "garage sale" every day of your life. Don't wait for the "rain" to remind you to enjoy the "sunshine.

PRESCRIPTION NO. 10

Don't take your life and loved ones for granted

- Every day, through your decisions and actions, you put a "price" on how much you value the people in your life.

- Don't wait for an unexpected "rain" or tragic turn of events to remind you that you may have undervalued your relationships.

- While the sun is still shining, tell your loved ones you love them.

CHAPTER 11

The Emperor's New Clothes Syndrome

Just as in the well-known children's fairy tale by Hans Christian Anderson, many people's lives reflect what I call "The Emperor's New Clothes Syndrome." You may remember the fellow who paraded down the street stark naked, yet everyone around felt obliged to comment on how beautifully he was dressed. No one wished to acknowledge the truth or, in this case, *the bare facts* of the situation.

If you are to make your life more like it could and should be, then you must be willing to objectively confront, evaluate and adjust, where necessary, the realities of your life. This is easier said than done. Too often, such objectivity can be very uncomfortable, and thus you may choose to avoid it. Sometimes you may engage in distortions of the truth, seeing primarily the good or primarily the negative, depending upon how you wish things to be. If you're not careful, you can become a writer of fiction, penning a story of your life that bears no resemblance to the facts but which satisfies your personal need to comply with some preconceived script that exists only in your mind. Your desire to fulfill your fantasies and dreams can be so strong that it totally overpowers your willingness or ability to see your life as it really is. Such selective vision can prevent you from exercising sound judgment.

For example, let's consider two people who meet and experience a physical and perhaps an emotional attraction. Let's assume that you are one of the parties involved. You want to be together because you feel some common bond, desire and chemistry. However, on a very fundamental level, your personalities, interests or needs, are just not compatible. Over time, these basic differences begin to surface, and it becomes more and more obvious to you or to the other party that your differences far outweigh your commonalties. You begin to argue, criticize, blame and resent each other, yet in your minds and hearts you desperately want this relationship to evolve into marriage. Either one or both of you begin to ignore or deny the major differences that exist in your relationship. Instead you idealize the relationship. Each time doubts begin to surface in you or the other party's conscious thoughts, they are quickly denied or rationalized away. Thus you may engage in selective reasoning so that truth and reality become what you choose to make them.

There are obviously real dangers in succumbing to "The Emperor's New Clothes Syndrome." If you do, you are exchanging the unpleasant long-term consequences of denying the facts of a situation for the short-term satisfaction of seeing it as you would like it to be. In short, your relationship is naked. You know it, but you act as if it were fully clothed.

This problem is very common in marriage. Once committed to a marital bond, spouses frequently refuse to acknowledge and recognize when there is a deterioration of the relationship. Assuming that there was an initial bond of love and affection at the time of courtship and marriage, the subsequent gradual drifting apart, loss of interest and/or respect for each other are either ignored or explained as a function of midlife crisis or career demands.

In most instances, nothing short of both parties getting involved in an effective marriage counseling program can salvage such a relationship. It is quite likely that through counseling, either or both will come to recognize that the origins of their conflicts may have their roots in "The Emperor's New Clothes Syndrome."

Through an open exchange of feelings, under the guidance of a trained professional, the individuals can begin to accept the realities of a situation and identify some options to revive or terminate the relationship. In either event, those involved will usually find that *it is easier and more fulfilling to live with the truth than to work hard at maintaining a fiction.* It clearly is hard work, on a day-to-day basis, to perpetuate and cling to a fantasy. There is a tremendous emotional, mental and physical expenditure of energy required in making, yourself and others believe an idealized, sometimes fabricated version of reality. This is not to say that you should never do this, for in fact that would be an almost impossible, unreasonable expectation to place on you. We all play the "Emperor's" game from time to time. The issue is really how often you play and on how grand a scale.

So I ask you to assess your own relationships, attitudes and beliefs about yourself and others and expose them to the light of truth. If, upon inspection, you find them in need of revision, then do so, but please exercise extreme caution. As stated earlier, the purpose of this book is not to lead you to become so disenchanted and disillusioned with what you find that you engage in a wholesale rejection and revision of your life. To do so would be foolhardy and self-defeating. The idea behind subjecting yourself and your life to closer scrutiny is to give you some insights into some *gradual adjustments* that might increase your level of personal satisfaction.

Please don't fall victim to a behavior pattern that became quite prevalent during the '60s and early '70s, when "tea group" encounters were quite popular. Some of you who are old enough may recall this reaction to total openness and "truth" as it was depicted in the movie, *Bob and Carol and Ted and Alice.* Even if you're too young to remember, I'm confident that you will get the point of this reference. The characters in the movie returned from an "encounter group" retreat that advocated total honesty, at all times and in all situations. Needless to say, the results were disastrous for their relationships. Their unprepared friends heard things that they were not ready for nor wanted to hear from Bob, Carol, Ted and Alice. Let's

THE EMPEROR'S NEW CLOTHES SYNDROME

not forget to use our common sense and good judgment when evaluating what we say and do. It's easy to get on an "honesty kick" that becomes so brutal and pervasive that it destroys rather than rebuilds personalities and relationships.

Let's face it: there are no people or relationships that couldn't stand a little improvement. Perfection is reserved for the Deity. By our very nature, we humans are destined to be flawed and imperfect, so keep in perspective your plan to make improvements. Don't become overzealous to remake the world or your life. You don't want to "throw the baby out with the bath water."

Remember, even in "The Emperor's New Clothes" there was a touch of humor as well as a lesson to be learned from the story. You don't always need to share the "naked truth" about a situation. Neither should you "dress" things up till it bares no resemblance to the truth. It's not wrong to acknowledge when a part of your life is really "naked." Such self honesty can be very liberating, and it will be your first step toward improvement. You may find that it is easier to correct it than to maintain a fiction.

PRESCRIPTION NO. 11

Be honest with yourself in appraising situations

- Have the courage to recognize that part of your life may not be as "clothed" as you would like.

- Recognizing your "nakedness" is the beginning of true growth and development.

- Accept the truth and use it as the foundation for building your relationships and making your decisions.

CHAPTER 12

Confucius Says,
"Don't Listen to Confucius"

No visit to a Chinese restaurant would be complete without the excitement of opening a fortune cookie. This tradition speaks to our curiosity and need to receive some mystical insight into what the future might bring. In matters of love, business, health, relationships and finance, why be logical and rational and rely on the outcome of our own efforts to influence the future when we can receive cryptic, unreliable but sage advice from a fortune cookie? Fortune cookies are more fun, though not any more accurate, than a horoscope, taro cards, palm reader, crystal ball, or tea leaves. In fact, sometimes the cookies are harder to swallow than the advice found within them.

Confucius Broder says, "People who look for easy answers to life will usually flunk the test." Life's answers cannot be found in a fortune cookie. Perhaps the only thing that you can gain from a fortune cookie is weight. Yet it is great fun to read one's fortune. Who knows? The baker may know something you don't. In any event, your life is far too important to relegate it to chance, luck and happenstance. Your life is the only one you have and you deserve the best, right? Therefore you must find ways to make your life work for you. This requires you to take responsibility, roll up your sleeves and actually get involved in making good things happen for you.

There's a saying: "Some people watch things happen, some people make things happen and some people don't even know what's happened." You must be a part of the group that makes things happen. Unfortunately life does not care what happens to you. Life is like a river that keeps flowing, regardless of what occurs in your life. Life was here before you were born, it is present now and, barring an unforeseen catastrophe, it will be here after you die. Life is not judgmental. It does not have preferences; it just exists for each of us to do with as we can.

If you wish to be happy you cannot ask life to make you happy. You cannot stand at your window each morning and call out, "Life, I want to be happy! I'm ready and waiting!" If you do so, you will not receive an answer. Rather than calling outwardly for some external force to do it for you, you must ask yourself these questions:

1. What do I want?
2. Why do I want it?
3. How can I go about getting it?
4. What price am I willing to pay to get it?

Then physically do what it takes and go after it! Or if you feel the price is too high, then leave it alone and move on.

There is no shortcut to happiness, health or success. *Wishing, dreaming and hoping only consume valuable time that should be used for working, acting and doing.* Accept the fact that you have the power and the tools to positively affect your life and the lives of others. You are a good person, and you should trust yourself to use this power.

Much of *your* life is what you *will* it to be! So much of what happens to you is really in your hands. So the next time you decide to choose one from Column A and one from Column B, make sure that you're choosing **action** and **commitment** dishes which will feed your life with the things you want. If you conclude your meal with a fortune cookie, be sure that you personally have filled it with a message of fact rather than hope.

PRESCRIPTION NO. 12

Take responsibility for your life

- Your future and your fortune cannot be found in a fortune cookie someone else has baked.

- Be the baker, determine the type of good fortune you want, secure the ingredients, mix the batter and then bake on high motivation and commitment for the rest of your life.

- You must provide the MSG: Motivation, Sacrifice and Grit! It will improve the taste of your life!

CHAPTER 13

Are You a Prisoner of Golden Handcuffs?

The expression "Golden Handcuffs" is frequently used when you are held captive to a situation that seems too good to leave but yet you find it also extremely dissatisfying. Perhaps it is a job that pays a good salary but also requires you, the employee, to put up with a supervisor who is obnoxious, inconsiderate and tyrannical. For you, every workday is filled with frustration, anxiety, pressure, tension and unhappiness. You have chosen to become a captive of money over happiness.

Could this really be your situation? Do you dread going to your job? If so, then getting out of bed, getting dressed and traveling to work is a really unpleasant experience for you because you know that much psychological and emotional pain awaits you. It's like preparing to go to the dentist for a root canal, only worse. Every day you fantasize about going to your boss and not only resigning, but in those eloquent words of the now- famous Johnny Paycheck song, you tell him to "take this job and shove it."

When all is said and done, however, you resist the temptation because you depend upon your salary and fringe benefits to maintain your current standard of living. You would like to change jobs, careers or at least supervisors, but you are unsure of your ability to do so successfully. You are restrained by fear, uncertainty, insecurity and, yes, the Golden Handcuffs. So you resign yourself to suffer and be unhappy for more than three hundred days a year, eight hours a day for as many years as remain until you retire.

Those invisible restraints, the Golden Handcuffs are ever present in many personal as well as business relationships. How many marriages today are characterized by one or both of the partners feeling that they are merely "hanging in," "tolerating" or "making the best" of a mediocre situation? The partner or partners stay together because the relationship fills certain financial needs, security needs, parenting needs, appearance needs and/or out of habit or convenience. Saddled with the responsibilities of a big mortgage, extensive personal property, school-age children, "appearances" for business and the community and a host of other "links," the Golden Handcuffs bind many a spouse to a relationship that is less than satisfying.

It's almost like the "pleasure-pain principle" of life. If the perceived pleasure of a situation or relationship is greater and/or more tolerable than the perceived pain of change, then one accepts the situation. If the fears, insecurities and disorientation that frequently accompany divorce are more dreaded than the day-to-day arguments, romantic voids and unmet needs of a given marriage, then you may opt to stay in the relationship. In essence, you are being held by Golden Handcuffs when you fear risking the loss of the goose that keeps laying golden eggs even though half the eggs may be rotten.

In your life, you may feel trapped, restrained or boxed in to a situation that meets some of your needs at the expense of many others. You may find it difficult to work up the courage to make changes or take risks to improve things for fear of losing what you already have. Perhaps you are reasoning, "Half a loaf is better than none" or "Why trade away the known for the unknown?" It's possible that a strong case can be made to justify this position. Only you can really evaluate what's best for you. However, I'm urging you to really take an honest, hard look at any situation or relationship that you're merely tolerating because it has some good but at the same time you feel is very detrimental to your physical or emotional health and happiness.

Here are some steps you can follow to assist you in deciding whether or not it would be to your benefit to free yourself from your personal Golden Handcuffs:

1. Clearly specify and identify the situation or relationship you wish to evaluate.

2. Write down what you currently are getting from that situation that is positive.

3. Write down what you don't like or what you feel is harmful to you about the situation.

4. In one column, put in priority or rank order, the positives; in another column, the negatives.

5. Place a 1–5 rating (with 1 being "totally unacceptable" and 5 being "very acceptable") next to each positive and each negative aspect of the situation.

6. Average the combined ratings for the pluses and minuses.

7. Analyze whether or not there are ways to increase the pluses and/or decrease the negatives without totally and radically leaving the situation.

8. Define your options for improving the situation.

9. Evaluate whether what's involved in improving the situation and the time frame associated with accomplishing it are doable and acceptable to you.

10. Evaluate whether or not you are paying too high a price, in terms of your health or happiness, to justify staying handcuffed to the situation.

11. Commit to **act to extricate yourself** or to **stay put**.

12. Write down your specific plan of action.

13. Implement and don't look back.

If you decide to "stay put," then make peace with yourself and the other parties involved and reconcile yourself to your decision. In short, make the best of your decision and approach it with a more positive attitude.

Let's apply these twelve steps to a fictional example:

STEP 1

I want to evaluate whether I should continue working for Company XYZ or seek a new job.

STEP 2

I receive the following benefits working for XYZ Company:
- above-average salary
- health benefits
- retirement program
- two weeks of paid vacation
- friendship of my coworkers

STEP 3

I don't like the following about working for XYZ Company:
- I have to work long hours (60) with no extra pay
- I have to work every Saturday and one Sunday a month
- I have only have a small desk in a tiny cubicle
- I have too much paperwork
- My supervisor is an insensitive tyrant who makes me feel unappreciated and incompetent
- It takes me one hour each way to travel to work in heavy traffic

STEP 4 AND STEP 5

Positives	Negatives
Salary – 4	Long hours – 1
Health benefits – 5	Weekend work – 1
Retirement – 4	Supervisor – 1
Friendship – 4	Cramped work environment – 1
Vacation – 4	Travel time – 2
	Paperwork – 2

STEP 6

On a 1–5 scale of satisfaction, the average score for my current job is 2.6, which indicates considerable dissatisfaction.

STEP 7

Short of quitting my job, the only change I can see is to ask for a transfer to another location. This would mean exchanging my current friends for the opportunity to have a new supervisor who may or may not be better than my current one. However, I don't see any ways of improving those other negatives, short of quitting.

STEP 8 AND STEP 9

Although I dread the prospect of hunting for a new job. I am very unhappy and I'm beginning to exhibit physical ailments such as high blood pressure, headaches and fatigue, which might be caused or exacerbated by my present job. What good is a retirement plan and a good salary if I don't live to enjoy them? I guess I'm paying too high a price for the financial security that this job provides.

STEP 10

Tomorrow I will discreetly but actively begin looking for a new job. However, I won't quit this one until I find a new one.

STEP 11 AND STEP 12

I will start looking in the want ads, networking with friends and contacting headhunters.

Even if you choose not to follow this process per se, it is important that you periodically evaluate various aspects of your life. There is nothing to be gained by exhibiting a martyr complex and unnecessarily enduring in silence because you feel chained and victimized by circumstances.

Golden Handcuffs usually retard your ability to grow and pursue greater happiness. These invisible bonds usually deceive and delude you into overestimating what you currently have and what you might have to sacrifice should you break loose and seek the freedom to pursue greener pastures. The longer you wait, the harder it is to put the key in the lock and turn it. No intelligent person should sentence herself to her own personal prison. However, don't knee-jerk your reaction without first carefully thinking through your options and the consequences that will follow. Make sure you are prepared and committed to your decision.

PRESCRIPTION NO. 13

Don't Be a Captive of "Golden Handcuffs"

- "Golden handcuffs" are made of emotion, not steel.

- They are tempered by fear of the unknown and by uncertainty and doubt.

- The key to unlock them is made of reason, self-honesty and hope.

- Have the courage to turn the key.

- Remember, there is a difference between real gold and "fool's gold."

CHAPTER 14

Even Babe Ruth Had a Batting Slump!

Professional athletes, be they soccer players, cricket players, football, basketball or baseball players, periodically find themselves in a performance slump. To use baseball to make the point, even the best baseball hitter periodically goes into a batting slump. When this happens, the "slumping" player often engages in certain behaviors that can plunge him into an even more prolonged slump. There are some parallels between what happens to the hitter and what happens to everyday people, like you, when you find yourself in a personal or professional "slump."

Let's first look at the baseball player's predicament. One day he's tearing the cover off the ball and hitting almost every pitch thrown at him. His batting average moves above .300, which for baseball is bordering on stardom, and his confidence level is sky high. Even the media starts giving him a lot of attention. The fans in the stands applaud and cheer for him every time he comes to bat, and his teammates pat his backside and let him know how glad they are to have him around.

However, as you have probably learned by now, most things in life come and go in cycles, and so, too, one day our batting star begins to find the magic fading. He starts striking out more, his swing is off, his batting average begins to dip, the fans stop cheering, the media stops covering him or they begin to cover him in a critical manner, and his teammates begin to avoid him in the dugout. "How could this happen?" he asks. "What can I do about it, and fast?" he asks his coaches.

Panic and loss of confidence begin to set in. He is determined to stop this terrible turnaround of events, so he tries harder and harder each time he steps up to bat. In fact, he wants to get a hit so badly that his over-eagerness to succeed begins to overpower his sense of timing and good judgment. Our "fallen star" begins to swing at bad pitches. He begins to question whether he has forever lost his hitting talents. He begins to worry about being traded, being relegated to sitting on the bench or being sent down to the minor leagues.

The harder he tries, the deeper he falls into his slump. Alas, all seems lost until one of the coaches calls him aside, puts his hand around his shoulder and calmly says, "Son, you have the talent to hit or you would never had made it to the major leagues. We've all seen how well you can hit because you've done it before. What you're going through is very common and it will pass. The best thing you can do is to *relax, stop pressing so hard* and go back to the fundamentals of where to stand and how to swing the bat. *Practice and patience* will help you turn this slump around."

Let's take a look at the parallel of this illustration to your life. By virtue of being an adult, at least based upon your chronological age, you are playing the "Game of Life" in the "Major Leagues." You are not an amateur, you are a professional You must have already demonstrated that you are able to hit what is thrown at you, at least to an acceptable degree, since you are still in the game. Your prognosis to survive and to thrive, both professionally and personally, depends upon your ability to get "hits." Now, in life, as in the game of baseball, there are periods when you go into a "slump." Things just aren't going right for you. There's either illness, a disappointment in love, loss of job, financial problems, etc., which all seem to hit you at the same time.

You feel overpowered by events, and you begin to question your ability to cope. Just like the batter, you too can become overanxious. You begin to "press" and try too hard, usually with disappointing results. You begin to forget how to be a "hitter," and you begin to forget the fundamentals that were responsible for many of your previous successes. In short, you feel as if you've been programmed to "strike out." What can or should you do? I recommend the following steps:

1. Accept the fact that this is part of a normal cycle of successes and failures that occurs in life. It comes with the territory.
2. Get mentally prepared to ride it out. Don't assume a "victim" mentality.
3. Be extra patient.
4. Don't panic and begin to try too hard.

5. Go back to those fundamental attitudes and behaviors that were previously successful for you.

6. Find your own "coach" to pat you on the back and to be your support system during your slump.

7. Stay in the game and keep taking swings.

Please remember that even in baseball no one consistently hits .1000, .500, .400, or even .350. In fact, a great batting average is anything above .300. This means that even the great baseball players get a hit only a little less than once out of every three times at bat.

Why, then, in life do you perhaps set some unrealistic expectations as to how many hits you should get to feel good about yourself? Can you be happy getting a hit only once in every three times at bat in life's game? More importantly, are you willing to suit up every day knowing in advance that you will be striking out, getting thrown out, making errors, getting dirty, possibly getting hurt but also getting a few hits along the way? The ability to get out of a slump usually begins with your attitude. Take a step back, evaluate what's really going on, and develop a plan that will take you back to the common-sense fundamentals of thinking and acting. Try to be philosophical about your slump and say to yourself "This too shall pass," and most of the time it will.

PRESCRIPTION NO. 14

Use a positive attitude and common sense to get out of a "slump"

- Keep in perspective what is really going on in your life.

- Be a player, not a spectator.

- Some good things and some bad things will happen during the game.

- Be grateful for the opportunity to play.

- Improve your attitude, take a step back, analyze what's causing the slump and address the source of the problem.

- Sometimes you *will* need to consult a "coach."

CHAPTER 15

Disappointments Are Not Tragedies

In life it is impossible not to experience periodic disappointments, setbacks and at times a feeling of total devastation regarding your goals, hopes, expectations, aspirations and relationships. You lose a business deal, sale or commission. Your boyfriend, girlfriend, spouse or friend deserts you for another. The death of a loved one leaves you totally distraught. The shock, pain and hurt that accompany these tumultuous events often seem unbearable. The temptation and natural reaction is to throw up your hands in surrender and defeat and cry, "Why go on?"

If you lose a major business deal, you may doubt another one will ever come along. The money you were counting on, and which had been spent numerous times in your mind for things you wanted, has suddenly disappeared. If you are rejected by a loved one, you are sure that somehow you failed or were found undesirable. Guilt, anger, and a feeling of being totally "crushed" into utter despair permeates your mind and body. You ache with both physical and emotional pain. The possibility of recovering and rebounding from your loss seems remote and highly unlikely.

It is at times such as these that you must force yourself to think of and recite two important sayings: "This too shall pass" and "Keep your problems in perspective." Disappointments are easier to rebound from than tragedies, yet frequently we make the mistake of classifying all disappointments as tragedies. For example, the loss of a business deal, while a disappointment, does not preclude your ability to ever make another deal again. However, if you were to suffer a massive stroke or other major debilitating physical condition that would permanently impair your ability to think or act, then and only then could you forget about ever making another deal again. That, my friend, is a tragedy! If your loved one leaves you, there is always the possibility of reconciliation. If your loved one dies, you have no future, only memories. The death of a loved one is an irreversible and irreplaceable situation. That qualifies as a tragedy!

As a rule, it is somewhat easier to apply the "This too shall pass" and "Keep your problems in perspective" remedies to disappointments as opposed to tragedies. In either event, it is often important for you to find an explanation to justify the disappointment or tragedy. You often engage in a variety of complicated, soul-searching "mental gymnastics" to find the "why, how and what": "Why did this happen to me? How could this happen to me? What did I do to deserve this fate?" All these are legitimate, expected reactions to unacceptable, painful events as you try to cope with life's curveballs and make sense out of the experience. When life pitches you a ball that you can't hit and you feel that you have "struck out," then you need a reason to justify your summoning up the courage to come to bat again.

As long as the answers you find are not self-destructive, self-inflicted guilt wounds, then the need to find some answer is appropriate and understandable and usually helpful. Everyone needs some time to recover from an emotional shock, but no one can afford to wallow for long periods of time in despair, grief, and self-pity. Like that river that keeps flowing whether or not you are present, life doesn't care whether or not you are happy or sad, wealthy or poor, good or bad. To a large degree, your own situation really depends, on what you, and you alone, choose to make it, so the sooner you work through your disappointment or tragedy, the sooner you actively do something to break out of your despair, the sooner you will be able to move on with your life.

The practical bottom line of life is the imperative to live, to move on and to make the very best with what you have to work with. Saying it is easy. Doing it is often very hard – but the alternative is unacceptable. The important thing is to not overdramatize and overreact to a situation that is unwanted or unexpected. There are times to be disappointed, times to be discouraged, and times to be legitimately devastated. If you don't differentiate among those situations in your reactions to them, then you are not being intellectually and emotionally honest with yourself, and you will most likely alienate people who could be part of your support group.

PRESCRIPTION NO. 15

React to each adversity in proportion to its severity

- There is a definite difference between a disappointment, a setback and a tragedy. The depth and intensity of your response should reflect the reality of each situation.

- Evaluate the situation objectively.

- Don't overreact.

- Adopt a "survivor" mentality.

- After adversity, move forward with your life as quickly as possible. *What's the alternative?*

CHAPTER 16

Reading Your Dashboard of Life

Thank goodness for the dashboard on your car! How many times has it saved you untold aggravation, expense and potential disaster? Your car has just been washed. It's clean and shiny. The sky is clear, and, from all you can determine, things at the moment are going well. You're driving down the highway. Suddenly a dashboard light comes on that says, "engine" or "oil" or "battery."

Being a rational person, you don't dismiss the message but rather it immediately monopolizes your thinking. First you probably realize, *I must have a problem with this car. I better get it checked out as soon as possible.* The last thing I want is to break down at 1 a.m. on some isolated road on a rainy night. You make that message on your dashboard a priority on your to-do list. You decide on the appropriate mechanic to take your car to, and you get as early an appointment as possible. Hopefully it is diagnosed as a minor problem involving a minimum of expense and a minimum of disruption in your life. You know that you had no choice but to respond quickly to that dashboard message and are grateful that the car was designed with dashboard warning lights.

Well, if you think about it, you also have an invisible "dash-

DOES YOUR LIFE NEED A LAXATIVE?

board" in your life, which is constantly blinking warning lights to you as well. There are lights blinking at work, in your personal relationships, in social relationships and in your body, all alerting you to potential problems, dangers and breakdowns. Unfortunately you are too often either oblivious to these "warning lights" in your life or you choose to ignore them, and thus you get yourself into unnecessary trouble.

Let's examine this concept of the "dashboard" in more specific terms. One day your spouse tells you that he wants a divorce. You are stunned, shocked, in total disbelief at what he just said. "How could this be? I didn't see this coming! I didn't know you were so unhappy. This is unbelievable!" Well, in all likelihood, this is not unbelievable, and you should have seen it coming. Perhaps if you had been alert to the "dashboard lights" it wouldn't have come to this. There were signs. You just chose to ignore them. Didn't you notice that there was less laughter, more arguments, fewer romantic interludes, less time spent together, greater "distance" between you? You chose to ignore, dismiss and or deny the dashboard lights.

Or you are called in by your boss and told that you are being let go. Again you register shock, disbelief and indignation at this unexpected act of forced separation. Come on, now, don't act so naïve! There were lights probably flashing for some time that either signaled financial problems with the company, requiring cutbacks, or dissatisfaction with your performance, as evidenced by the evaluations you received, comments made to you, your exclusion from important meetings, a change in whom you report to or being passed over for a promotion. **Those were the dashboard lights!**

You are at home working on your computer when suddenly you feel a numbness in your left arm and excruciating pressure on your sternum. It feels like an elephant is walking on your chest. The next thing you know, you are calling 911, an ambulance is whisking you to the hospital and you find yourself in the emergency room, where you are told that you had a heart attack. "How could this be? I had no symptoms, no warning, no reason to be concerned." **Oh, yes you did!** You had those warning lights on your body's "dashboard" blinking at you for months, if not years. Remember the lab report that indicated you had an elevated cholesterol level? Remember your doctor giving you the same message for the last five years, to "lose weight, exercise, stop smoking, switch to a low fat diet? **Those were your lights, but you chose to ignore them!**

The analogy should be very clear to you. You are constantly receiving feedback of one kind or another that you should view as your personal set of warning lights. They are trying to protect and shield you from disastrous consequences in various areas of your life. Your willingness or unwillingness to acknowledge them will determine the quality of your relationships and your life.

Here are some simple steps to help you benefit from the "dashboard" philosophy:

1. Understand and accept the concept and analogy of having a "dashboard of life."
2. Consciously tune in to feedback you receive from others and situations, and ask yourself if you are experiencing a blinking light.
3. Try to analyze what triggered the light and what it is saying to you.
4. Go to the source of the problem.
5. If necessary, see a psychological "mechanic."
6. Consider the implications, for you, of adjusting your behavior and thoughts to accommodate those lights.
7. Periodically review your decision to see if it was the correct one and if it is still relevant.
8. Share the "dashboard" concept with someone you care about.

PRESCRIPTION NO. 16

Monitor and respond to your dashboard of life

- You were given the gift of dashboard lights in your life.

- To avoid breaking down on your highway of life, monitor them and heed them.

- Keep your eyes focused more on your dashboard and less on your accelerator.

CHAPTER 17

Life's a Gas!

There is no question that we all depend on gasoline for fueling our cars and fueling our respective life styles. Periodically, international crises or natural disasters may cause gas prices to rise. As the consumer, you have little choice but to either cut back on your consumption of gas, buy a car that gets better miles per gallon and/or pay whatever the supply-and-demand price is at the pump. At the pump you are typically offered a choice of three octane levels: 87, 89 or 93. The selection you make determines the final price per gallon you pay. Although we are told that there is a qualitative difference in each choice, the reality is that any of the three octanes will enable your car to get you where you want to go, with varying degrees of efficiency.

To apply this analogy to your life, each of you has a choice of the "octane" you choose to put in your "engine of life." Some of you may have been consciously or unconsciously selecting a low octane level of effort, enthusiasm and commitment. Some of you may have been filling up with a medium level of commitment, enthusiasm, passion, planning, etc. Some of you may have selected the premium octane and, though you are paying a higher price in terms of time, sacrifice and effort, it is allowing you to tool down the road of life, hitting all the sites you want to see and, for the most part, having a great trip.

Similarly, choices that you make in life will keep you moving, but unlike with your car, there are significant differences in the consequences, results and outcomes you experience when you make your selection from the "octanes of life." In your life, it should not be just a matter of whether you are going somewhere or anywhere, it is a matter of going where you want to go on the road that you want to travel and arriving when you want to arrive. Accomplishing this objective will often require you to fill up with the higher octane gas. There is a saying that some people aim at nothing in life and hit it with amazing accuracy. That saying reflects a low-octane approach to life.

Let's first look at the ingredients contained in each "octane." One ingredient takes the form of *nutritional, health and wellness composition.* Do you get adequate sleep and eat a well-balanced, healthy diet as opposed to fast-food junk? Do you exercise or are you sedentary?

Another ingredient includes your *attitudinal, mental and emotional make-up.* Are you positive, optimistic, full of passion and enthusiasm or do you expect the worst and live each day as if it were a trip to the dentist? Do you value your abilities, your potential and yourself? Do you like and accept your appearance, physical limitations, health restrictions, family dynamics and personality? Do you understand yourself—your needs, idiosyncrasies and tolerance levels? Do you understand your work ethic and level of "hunger" that motivates you to get what you want?

Then there is the ingredient of *personal and professional goals, dreams and aspirations.* What do you want to achieve in terms of relationships, marriage, lifestyle and career objectives? Have you clearly and specifically defined for yourself your values, priorities and career goals?

Think of your life as an engine that runs on "gas." You must go to that the pump on a regular basis to fill up your emotional, physical and psychological engine. Each person varies in how many miles per gallon she can get on her tank before she needs another fill-up. A fill-up may take the form of a vacation, quiet time, exercise, meditation, etc. The better care you take of your emotional, spiritual, intellectual and physiological health, the farther you can go before another fill-up is needed. The problem for many people, and the frustration and disappointment they experience, occurs when they are filling up with a low octane but the goals they have set for themselves require high octane.

There are many ingredients to consider and questions to ask before you select your octane level. Everyone does not and should not select the "high octane." It's okay to select the low or medium octane as long as it is consistent with the goals you have defined for yourself. For example, if you want to live in a cabin in a remote area and pretty much live off the land, you will do fine with the low-grade octane. However, if you want a million-dollar home plus a beach house, two sports cars and memberships in exclusive country clubs, then you better fill up with the high octane. You better be ready, willing and able to commit with passion the bulk of your time, energy and psyche to that goal and be prepared to pay the price of sacrifice that comes with it. So get your map, decide where you want to go, fill up your "emotional tank" with the right octane gas, fasten your seat belt and enjoy the ride of your life—'cause life's a gas!

PRESCRIPTION NO. 17

Choose the octane level that you need to get where you want to go

- Decide where you want to go.

- Determine how you plan to get there.

- Identify the level of "octane" you need, and know where to find the gas pumps.

- Be sure you can afford the fill-up.

CHAPTER 18

Do You Still Ride the Merry-Go-Round?

It was a fun ride; it was a safe ride; it was a fantasy ride. When you were a child, it was sheer delight to ride the merry-go-round, with the wooden horses moving rhythmically up and down the gold poles to the sound of music emanating from the big calliope. "Please can I ride again?" was your standard plea to your parents. There were never enough "agains" to satisfy you. As you would go round and round, you would always stretch to try to capture the brass ring. During your early childhood years that ring was usually just beyond reach, but as you matured it was very satisfying to collect a ring with each cycle of the ride.

I associate a merry-go-round with innocence and fun. For me, it symbolizes an oasis from the complexities and stresses of contemporary life. It is a time capsule of wonderful memories that, when the opportunity presents itself, you can open for five or ten minutes. It is the safest ride, it is the tamest ride, and in some respects it is the most boring ride, but it still satisfies a need.

Figuratively, in the "Amusement Park of Life" there are many rides from which you can choose. There are rides that vary in motion, speed, risk, intensity and safety. There are some rides that are age appropriate and you must be a certain height, age or weight to be able to ride them. There are rides that warn that being pregnant or such health problems as heart disease should disqualify you from participating. There are rides that require you to be strapped in, rides you share with another individual, in the same car, and there are group rides. Some rides can make you nauseated; some can leave you laughing hysterically. So, too, some will make you scream with fear.

The question is: Have you graduated from riding the merry-go-round? Have you matured enough to try some of the other, more daring and demanding rides in the Amusement Park of Life? If not, why not? Has it not become obvious to you that the real brass rings of life are not to be found on the merry-go-round?

With all due respect to nostalgia, there is no harm in your occasionally buying a ticket to the preferred ride of your childhood. There are days and times in your life when a calmer ride will get you what you want. Especially when you pursue spiritual goals, the merry-go-round may be the ride of choice. There is nothing inherently wrong or inappropriate with this safe, more methodical approach.

However, if you want to pursue a goal that requires risk, sustained intensity and commitment, passion, zeal or creativity, then the merry-go-round is not the ticket to buy. In such instances, you should walk around the Amusement Park of Life and find a roller coaster, Tilt-A-Whirl, Scream Machine or the like. **In short, take a more daring approach to achieving your goal. Don't always play it safe!** If you are emotionally and physically healthy, if you are sufficiently mature, if you a serious about achieving your dreams and goals, then you must act and think like an adult. **Be brave! Be a risk taker! Be assertive! Be courageous!**

Perhaps the reason your marriage or your job is bland, repetitive and boring is that you live it as if you were riding a merry-go-round. Perhaps some of your important dreams are still unfulfilled because of your unwillingness to pursue them with intensity, enthusiasm and a willingness to face your fear by riding that ride you never dared to ride as a child. When was the last time you allowed your heart to race, allowed your voice to scream, challenged your fear and strapped yourself in for the ride of your life? Only you, in your adult heart of hearts, know whether you have graduated from the safe, monotonous, predictable and childish attraction of the merry-go-round. So, if you have not already done so, step right up and experience the ride of your life!

PRESCRIPTION NO. 18

Ride as many rides as possible in the amusement park of life

- Ride all the rides in the "Amusement Park of Life."

- Each ride will help you to achieve a different goal.

- Make sure that you're emotionally old enough and healthy enough for the rides you select.

- Don't limit yourself to the safe, familiar merry-go-round.

- Allow yourself to experience the fear, the fun, the rush of new rides.

CHAPTER 19

Are You Willing to Milk Your Cow?

If you know anything about exercising, then you have heard the "mantra" of most exercise instructors and most people who exercise: **"No pain, no gain!"** There is a great deal of truth in that statement. To extend the exercise analogy further, you will find that most things worth having in life will require "blood, sweat and tears." While the dreamers, talkers and non-achievers in life waste their time and energies looking for the easy path to achieving their goals, the achievers know, either through personal experience or common sense, that with few exceptions, there are no easy roads to success.

To resort to additional clichés, "There is no substitute for hard work" and "There is no free lunch." Now, to be realistic, being virtuous, dedicated and a hard worker will not necessarily result in success. We all know people who have those characteristics and they still never achieve their goals, so I like to say, **"Hard work will not guarantee success, but lack of hard work will almost certainly guarantee failure."**

Many people prefer to delude themselves, and others, by going through the motions of pursuing their goals. It's like a person buying the most expensive jogging shoes and workout outfit, and then limiting their use to wearing them while walking around the house, neighborhood and supermarket. That person will never shed a pound nor strengthen a muscle, but he will try to create the impression that he has made a commitment to physical fitness.

How committed are you to doing whatever is necessary to achieve your goals? Are you willing to work hard, exercise the self-discipline and make the sacrifices necessary to get what you want? We are now talking about the issue of **motivation**, which literally means **"move to action."** If you're hungry enough for something, if you want something badly enough, then I submit that you qualify as a motivated person.

I often receive calls from individuals inviting me to come and motivate their employees, managers, students, etc. My standard response is that I cannot motivate anyone other than myself, and even that at times is a difficult job. All that I can do is provide people with insight as to the concept of motivation. But in the final analysis, a person must experience, within himself, a burning cauldron of inner fire that cannot be extinguished until his objective is achieved.

To be strong enough to sustain an individual's drive and energies long enough to achieve an objective, motivation must come from within. External motivation helps one get the kerosene and match, but internal motivation will get you to start the fire and to keep it burning. Motivation for an objective is not a sometime thing. It is an every-minute thing. If you're truly motivated, then you become like a heat seeking missile pursuing your target. You will not allow anything from diverting your focus from your goal.

There is a saying, "Cows don't give milk, you've got to take it." No farmer wakes up in the morning and hears a voice coming from the barn saying, "Yoo-hoo, Farmer Brown, I have some milk waiting for you in the bucket." That farmer must get out of bed while it's still dark, and perhaps damp and cold. He may be tired, but he forces himself to dress, go out in the cold, go to the barn and take the milk from the cow.

In life, the people who tend to achieve their goals are the Farmer Browns of the world. While the rest of the folks roll over in bed because they want to sleep and don't want to go out in the cold to milk their "cow," the achievers, those who succeed, behave like Farmer Brown. Are you a "roll over, pull up the covers and stay warm" person or are you a Farmer Brown?

It's important never to begrudge or envy another's accomplishments because in most instances he was willing to do things that you were unwilling to do. Celebrate his success! Rejoice in his accomplishment! Admire his tenacity! He earned it!. Be honest with yourself as to the reasons why you may have not experienced a similar success.

Most of us know people who are highly positive, upbeat and what might be termed "highly motivated." So, too, we know people who are such negative gloom-and- doomers that no matter what situation they find themselves in, they will always find something negative to complain about. It's like the negative lady who won $2 million in the lottery and upon notification of her good fortune immediately responded, "Yes, but I'll have to pay taxes on it."

When you think about how to become motivated, it's as much a matter of avoiding people who will de-motivate you as it is surrounding yourself, personally and professionally, with people who are themselves highly motivated and upbeat people who will sustain and support your own level of motivation. Both positivism, as well as negativism, are contagious. Be a carrier of positivism.

PRESCRIPTION NO. 19

Increase your tolerance for sacrifice to achieve what you want

- Life works on the "pleasure-pain principle."

- If you want something badly enough, then you'll endure the pain.

- You have a higher "pain threshold" than you think.

- Be honest with yourself as to what you really want and how badly you want it. The motivation will follow.

- Never begrudge others their successes. They earned it.

- Be like Farmer Brown and be willing to milk your cow.

CHAPTER 20

You're Never Too Old for Your "Blankie"

Did you have a "blankie," that thing that started out as a full-blown blanket that was probably given to you as a gift at birth? Somehow, from amongst all the blankets you were given, it became your favorite. You loved its touch, its texture; you loved its smell. It became an inseparable part of you. Wherever you went, you insisted that your "blankie" come along. It made you feel safe. It was your constant source of security and comfort. You slept with it, ate with it, crawled with it, played with it. You suffered separation anxiety whenever your mom, to give it that much needed wash, took it away from you.

As the years passed, your "blankie" became tattered, shredded and shrunken, but its loss of size in no way diminished its value for you. Whatever remnant of it that survived still was your best friend. But eventually there came a the time when you no longer wanted to be seen in public with your "blankie." It would have been embarrassing. So you went "undercover," figuratively and perhaps literally, by clandestinely spending time with your "blankie" in the privacy of your room. If you became anxious, frustrated, hurt or disappointed you could always retreat to the cocoon of your "blankie." You still slept with it, but no one knew but you. As you matured from toddler to adolescent to young adult, your "blankie" discreetly shared this personal journey with you. In private, you still experienced the joy and comfort of fondling, sniffing and caressing your faithful "blankie."

But alas, adulthood blindsided you, and you soon found yourself a twenty-, thirty-, forty- or fifty-plus-year-old grownup who would surely become a recipient of concern, ridicule and significant social consequences should you persist with any visible attachment to your "blankie." You couldn't risk ever being caught with your unconditional, always reliable, always there for you best friend, your "blankie." The time had regrettably arrived for the final separation, so that tattered remnant of comfort, security and emotional reverie was forever laid to rest in some box or closet, never to be touched, caressed or fondled again. Your "blankie" days were over!

However, the personal needs that it satisfied for you did not go away. Every so often, even now, as an adult, you may still experience moments of vulnerability, self-doubt, indecision, hurt and frustration. You still need and yearn for a "blankie" substitute. You may have sought this substitute through relationships with spouses, family, friends, work, organizational activities, spiritual involvement and the like. Hopefully, in your quest for security, you have not tried to replace your "blankie" with addictive behaviors involving alcohol, drugs, gambling extra-marital affairs or other forms of abusive and self-destructive behavior.

To varying degrees, your relationships may have helped but you still probably wish that your life were less stressful and that you didn't feel the need, as often as you do, for a "blankie." By its very nature and design, life creates situations for you when the stresses, responsibilities, expectations and decisions that you confront can understandably, at times, be very difficult to handle. You still may need a substitute "blankie" of some kind to help you initially manage, cope and, hopefully, ultimately thrive in your life.

Regardless of your age, background, sex or other demographic criteria, the common denominator is that you would really benefit if you could create greater peace of mind, more happiness and fulfillment in your life. This would significantly cut down on your need for the proverbial "blankie,"

So as an adult what are your options when it comes to the issue of finding an effective and acceptable "blankie" substitute? First, don't sell yourself short. Recognize and remind yourself that you are a worthwhile individual. You may be less than perfect, but you are far from defective. Pay yourself an emotional "visit" and bring yourself a "housewarming" gift, the gift of acceptance and appreciation.

Now, although at first glance this may sound like a glib cliché, the fact is that sometimes you really need to look within yourself to find the inner strength necessary to persevere in the face of adversity. Too often you may have gotten in the habit of looking for external "blankies" that often offer limited help. There are times that you just have to "suck it up" and look within yourself for the strength, the energy and the backbone needed to get through a situation.

You have talent, you have intellect, you have compassion, you have humor, you have curiosity, you have creativity, you have experience, and the list goes on. The greatest part of your inner emotional "blankie," the strongest thread in its composition is that you are still alive and you still have life, breath and the opportunity to make decisions that can positively impact yourself and others.

Don't allow yourself to wallow in self-pity, whining and self-centered "poor me" behavior. Resist the temptation to revert to your infantile behavior that is no longer necessary and in fact is counterproductive. Your psyche coupled with whatever external support system of relationships you have developed can and should become your adult "blankie.". Revisit memories that remind you of your successes, your strength, your wisdom, and then feed off of them to provide you the security and support you need at the moment. Remember, you are never too old for your "blankie," but your "blankie should now be your self-confidence and feeling of self-worth.

PRESCRIPTION NO. 20

Toughen up! Use your inner strength as your adult "blankie"

- Whether you're eight months or eighty years old, it is normal to need and want a sense of security.

- As you get older, replace the tangible "blankie" you used as a child with your own personal emotional "blankie" made from memories of past accomplishments and recognition of your inherent worthiness as a human being.

- Remember ILAC: "I am lovable and capable."

- Come on, now—toughen up!

CHAPTER 21

Are You a Disciple of Ben Franklin?

Benjamin Franklin is credited with counseling us, "Don't put off for tomorrow what you can do today." Many of us seem to act as if we think old Ben should have stuck to his kite flying and kept his nose out of the advice columns. After all, everyone knows that you should "put off until tomorrow whatever you can get away with"—right? Ask or observe any person who has a yard to mow, bills to pay, a term paper to write, taxes to calculate or any other less-than-pleasant task to perform. Delay, procrastination and avoidance are the typical behaviors with which you tend to approach unpleasant chores and responsibilities. The tendency is to wait for the very last minute, until the deadline is staring you in the face and you have no choice but to tackle the task or face the consequences.

You might even contend that you do your best work under the pressures of an impending deadline or crisis. Somehow your creativity and the energy level needed for you to complete these "negative tasks" are released when your back is against the wall. As the sand in the hourglass speeds its descent to the bottom, as time rapidly runs out, your body, mind and spirit will seem to respond to the challenge of harnessing all the needed resources to beat the clock.

If this description is characteristic of how you respond to unpleasant tasks, then you're in good company. However, if you have dreams, goals and aspirations that are as yet unfulfilled, then please don't take comfort in being a member of the millions of procrastinators on this earth. If you do, then your dreams and goals may never be achieved, and they may become relegated to just your fantasy world. In that world, you would think about them as almost impossible to achieve. They would exist only for escaping from the more humdrum aspects of your life, and they would fall into the realm of your "someday, sometime, somehow" approach to making your dreams come true. Dreams can seldom if ever come true with such a nebulous, wishy-washy, non-specific approach.

Major aspirations fall into a very different category from such chores as mowing lawns, taxes and term papers. Each of these situations has an inherent, built-in deadline. At some point the grass will get so high that either you or your neighbors will know that it must be done; your teacher will set a date for completion of the assigned term papers, as will Uncle Sam for taxes and your creditors for your bills. These inherent deadlines will protect you from yourself and your tendency to procrastinate, and despite your own natural inclinations to delay, the tasks will eventually be accomplished.

But what if there are no deadlines? Then you have no defense against yourself. You are free to indefinitely put off doing whatever is needed to accomplish your goals. The tomorrow syndrome quickly takes over. You then do put off till tomorrow what should be done today. Procrastination becomes not only the "thief of time," but it also robs you of the possibility of realizing your dreams and goals.

What type of person are you? Are you part of the lucky minority that takes care of things well in advance of their deadlines, or are you part of the majority that acts only under the pressure of time? If in fact you are in the majority, then force yourself to set timeliness for the important things you want out of life. Intentionally place yourself under some pressure to act. Your chances of achieving what you want will be greatly increased.

For example, let's assume that you wish to own a larger, more expensive home. You find yourself mentally wishing, wanting, dreaming and fantasizing about this nicer home. You drive through neighborhoods that have your dream house, and you imagine what it would be like to live there. You may even have teased yourself by going into such a home, which is for sale, just to walk through and see what it looks and feels like from the inside. Thus far, you have gone through some good preliminary stages necessary for getting ready for getting what you want.

Next you think to yourself how much more income you would need to generate to own such a home. Then you consider ways you could earn that additional income. At this point, you really start looking with enthusiasm as you begin to see the possibilities for actually owning that dream home. Now you know what you want, you know approximately how much money it will take to get it and you have identified what you will have to do to generate the additional revenue. All that remains is to start doing some of these things.

This is where, unless you have stipulated a specific time by which you plan to own that dream home, your dream will crash in flames. Your habit of putting off doing what needs to be done takes over. Your own poor work habits begin to work against your ever getting that house. In the absence of creating artificial, self-imposed time pressures that you depend on to motivate you to act, you do nothing. Your dream house will always seem to elude you. You will feel frustrated and disappointed because the dream never seems to become reality. A major part of the explanation is your failure to have attached a timeline. You must set timelines and deadlines for accomplishing your goals and dreams so that a tendency to procrastinate does not become a serious handicap.

I can write about procrastination with some conviction because of my own tendency to be a procrastinator. The act of getting this book written is a perfect example. For several years, I planned to write this book, but I never set a timeline. Days, weeks and years passed without the first word ever having been written. Family, friends and members of audiences I have spoken to urged me to write this book. Intellectually and emotionally I agreed with them. I felt a strong desire and need to convey my ideas in writing, but I never set a timeline.

Then one day last year I came to the realization that my book would never be written unless I forced myself to exercise some self-discipline and set myself a deadline. D-day, for deadline day, was written in on my calendar for completion of the manuscript by April 2006 and publication by the summer 2006. However, this would be no April Fool's joke! Suddenly things began to happen. First I assembled pads and index cards, set up my word processor and made other preliminary arrangements. Then I began blocking out time for writing. Instead of reading on my flights between speaking engagements, I began using that time for writing. As the months went by and April 1, 2006, became more visible in my mind's eye and on the calendar, my writing pace picked up considerably. By April 2006 the final draft of my book was complete. As I looked at the finished manuscript, I experienced a tremendous feeling of personal satisfaction. I had accomplished my goal, achieved my dream and defeated the "thief of time."

You, too, can experience that feeling. You must do what I and millions of others of us procrastinators have to do: Force yourself to act by setting deadlines. Make Ben Franklin proud. The time is now!

Set deadlines for yourself

- There is a time to dream, but if you don't act on your dream by setting and meeting your deadlines, then your dream may become your nightmare or a mirage.

- Talk is cheap.

- Create structure, timelines, rewards and punishments to keep yourself on task.

- Understand the positive and negative consequences of what you do or don't do.

CHAPTER 22

Hey, Yogi!

"It's not over till it's over" is a line attributed to the great New York Yankee baseball player, Yogi Berra. This philosophical gem is as applicable to the game of life as it is to the game of baseball, for life is in fact a game, a competition between individuals and among all the human and environmental factors that impact on us. We each have a choice of playing the game aggressively, with daring, boldness and creativity, or we can stand on the sidelines as spectators, fantasizing what it would be like to get on the field and play. Obviously any player runs the risk of injury or a poor performance, but so too does he create the possibility of phenomenal personal satisfaction as he enjoys the thrill and excitement of the game.

Unlike some other games, the game of life is unique in that one is eligible to participate from that first breath of life to your final exhalation. It doesn't matter at any given point whether you're winning or losing or what is your age, your state of health, or your social or financial status. The sole object is to keep playing.

Don't give up, never throw in the towel, and never say, "I quit." There's no disgrace to fall behind in the score; we all do that from time to time. There's no shame in making errors, getting fatigued or even feeling down; we all do that from time to time. **But don't stop playing, and don't concede defeat.** Until such time as the final buzzer sounds, the final whistle blows, the last out in the ninth inning is made or the gun sounds signaling the official end of the game, each of us must keep playing to the best of our abilities.

As long as we stay in the game, we can retain that important ingredient of life, which is **hope.** Even in Greek mythology, when Pandora's box was opened and all the contents escaped from it, hope was the one thing that remained in the box. Hope is the ingredient that provides us with a sense of purpose. The importance of hope is best expressed in this poem:

The Optimist
by Richard Gunn

I passed a sand lot yesterday,
Some kids were playing ball.
I strolled along the third base line,
Within the fielder's call.

"Say, what's the score?" I asked the chap.
He yelled to beat the stuffin':
"There's no one out, the bases full
And they're forty-two to nuthin'!"

"You're gettin' beat, aren't you lad?"
And then in no time flat,
He answered: "No sir, not as yet!
Our side ain't been to bat!"

Yes, hope is the fuel that keeps us in the game. Hope allows us to believe that things will get better. We maintain hope that we can change circumstances more to our liking. Our hope that life will become increasingly more satisfying and fulfilling is what keeps us getting out of bed every day.

We all know young, healthy people whose day-to-day behavior reveals that they are no longer in the game. They may be addicts, dropouts, gang members, etc. They have no goals, no dreams, no feelings of connection with their fellow man. By the same token, we all know "old" people, chronologically old, that is, who are active, spunky, enthusiastic and involved players up until their last breath. You start the game crawling, then you walk, then you run and then you may limp, but regardless of your age, remember to keep your competitive spirit.

Many times people find excuses to justify not playing in the game of life. "I'm too old, I'm too poor, my bones ache." On and on the excuses fall from our lips, yet you periodically see physically handicapped people who overcome their obstacles to accomplish goals that you are reluctant to attempt. You meet immigrants to our country who overcome odds you don't have to contend with and who attain successes that surpass your own. So stop focusing on why you can't do whatever it is you want and emphasize what you *can* do!

It's like the old story of the women who said to her friend, "I wish I had gone to law school." Her friend responded, "Why don't you go to law school now?" "How can I?" asked the women, "I'm forty–seven years old!" Her friend asked, "Well, how long does it take to go to law school?" "Three years," answered the woman. "How old will you be at the end of law school, if you go?" inquired the friend. "Fifty years old," the woman replied. Her friend asked, "Well, how old will you be in three years if you don't go to law school?" You can see that the answer will be the same whether the woman goes to law school or not. So the point should be clear: Whatever your goal, just go for it!

Let me remind you that you get only one chance to play the game of life, so why not play it with all the gusto you can muster? Yogi Berra was right: "It's not over till it's over." You are obviously still breathing or you wouldn't be reading this book, so it's still not over for you!

PRESCRIPTION NO. 22

Never give up! Never give up!

- Remind yourself how good you are.

- As long as there is life, there is hope, but hope alone is not enough. You must also act.

- You have the power to fight adversity.

- Either win or go down fighting.

- Surrender is for cowards.

CHAPTER 23

Is Fear the Fuel That Drives Your Engine or Shuts It Down?

President Franklin D. Roosevelt, during World War II, said, "There is nothing to fear but fear itself." Those words sure make sense when you read them or hear them, but it's quite a different story when you experience the heart-wrenching feeling of fear in your own life. Fear is one of life's basic human instincts. Both humans and animals rely on that instinct to trigger an internal mechanism of alarm or alertness, a command to call all our senses "to man your battle stations" and be ready for action. Fear is part of your survival system and is designed to help you make the critical decision regarding perceived, impending danger. Should you fight or run?

Fear can transform you into an alert, high-strung "cat" ready to spring into action, or it can inject you with a chilling virus that spreads throughout your body, attacking and freezing all your muscles, thereby immobilizing you and making you incapable of response. Depending upon the given situation, each of us reacts differently to fear. However, there is no denying that fear is very much a part of life.

Rather than discuss fears that pose a physical danger, let's consider one specific type of fear, the fear of failure. It's natural for you to want to be successful. It's normal for you not to want to fail. Perhaps you are one of the people who may reason that the fear of dealing with the consequences and feelings of failure is greater than the sacrifices required to succeed. So you feel driven to succeed. You desire to experience the satisfaction and rewards of success. Thus the "pleasure-pain principle," which I mentioned in Chapter 13, dictates your behavior. Simply stated, if you perceive that you will derive more pleasure than pain in doing something, then you do it. If the reverse is true, then you avoid that activity.

The key word in that principle is "perceived." Your perception is your reality. If you perceive something as real, then it is real to you, regardless of whether or not it exists in reality. So, too, your perception of fear, as it relates to failure and its consequences, in any given situation, will usually influence your actions. Therefore it is important for you to analyze the accuracy of your perceptions regarding risk taking and its consequences.

Let me share a very real and personal experience of mine to demonstrate how I handled the fear that comes with taking risks. For fifteen years I worked as an educator and trainer for various school systems and organizations. During that time I received a reasonably good salary (by standards in the field of education), received generous health and retirement benefits, had an expense account and in general experienced a sense of professional respect, recognition and personal security. In addition, I was the sole support of my wife and three small children.

However, I had a burning desire to become an entrepreneur, to go out on my own and become a full-time professional speaker and trainer for businesses and organizations throughout the country. The risk of resigning my job and giving up the security and stability of a career built over fifteen years, which provided for the support of my family, seemed enormous. The more I contemplated the change and the more I shared my plan with people, the greater became the perceived risks and the more my fear elevated.

How could I justify jeopardizing the well-being of my family? What if I fell flat on my face? If I failed, would I be able to pick up the pieces? Was I really prepared to take the risk? How ready were my wife and family to accept the consequences of such a decision? On and on I pondered, generating more questions and more reasons why I should not take such a professional risk. The more I thought, the greater became my anxiety and fear of making such a decision.

Then I decided to check out my "perceptions" regarding what was looking increasingly like impending doom and disaster should I go ahead with such a decision. I asked myself six questions:

1. Why did I want to make this career change?
2. How strongly did I feel about making this change?
3. Did I really understand what was required to achieve success by pursuing this change?
4. Did I have the knowledge and competence required to make the change?
5. Was I, and my family, willing and able to make the required sacrifices?

6. What was the worst possible consequence that would occur if, at the end of one year, I totally failed in my new career?

These were the answers to my questions:

1. I was contemplating this change because I had a tremendous desire to apply what I felt to be strong speaking and training abilities into a new career.
2. I felt it would be more satisfying and lucrative, and I really believed in my abilities. I knew that I would always second guess myself and have regrets if I didn't pursue my dream.
3. I understood that I was starting from scratch and had to build a reputation and a significant account base to be successful.
4. I had the experience, training, and credentials required.
5. My wife and I had sufficient savings to underwrite our financial needs during this transition.
6. If, in fact, I was a total flop, then I knew that I had enough abilities and experience to be marketable and go back to work as an educator.

After rationally examining the issue, all visions of my wife selling apples and my children selling pencils on a street corner quickly vanished. I knew that I passionately wanted to make the change, and so, believing that I would not be financially or emotionally devastated should I fail, I developed a business plan that realistically outlined what would need to be done. The nice part about this story, and I believe most similar situations where people analyze their fears and relieve themselves of the pressures created by the fear of failure, is that it usually has a happy ending.

To provide balance to this discussion, let's acknowledge that, for some people, fear is a great motivator. Having served as a trainer of sales people for more than twenty years, I have met several salespeople who would intentionally commit to buying a house or car that they could not afford at the time and then use that financial commitment and the fear of not being able to afford it as their motivator to generate sales. They would create a situation in which they had their financial "backs against the wall," which forced them to perform. On the other hand, other salespeople allowed their fear to immobilize them, which led to financial and career devastation. Thus, depending on one's personality, the presence or absence of fear, and how one responds to it, fear can really be a two-edged sword.

Think about your own personality and history in dealing with fear. Have you been able to effectively respond in the face of adversity? It's important to remember that in life it doesn't matter how many times you get knocked down, but what does matter is how many times you get back up. Many a champion boxer has visited the canvas on numerous occasions. It is his ability to get back up and confront his adversary and eventually prevail that makes him a champion. You must be willing to get in the ring with your fears, be willing to take fear's best punch and perhaps get knocked down, but then stand up, look your fear in the eye and will it into submission.

PRESCRIPTION NO. 23

Confront and fight your fears

- If fear is your Goliath, then you must be the David. Take your slingshot, load up with rocks of belief in yourself and slay the giant!

- Your fear may not fall on the first shot, but over time you can wear it down.

- As big and scary as a fear may be in your mind, it is much less harmful to you than the feelings you will live with every day if you remain intimidated.

CHAPTER 24

Don't Treat Allies Like Invaders

Has there been at least one time in your life when you felt as if you were drowning in an emotional crisis? It may have been the death of a loved one, a catastrophic illness, marital or family conflict, loss of a job, or just a period of unexplainable depression. The emotional drain was probably enormous, and you might have wondered whether you would survive the crisis. In your weaker moments perhaps even thoughts of suicide as a way out may have crept into your consciousness.

Even the most levelheaded person is not immune to succumbing to such feelings of pressure. If and when you ever find yourself sinking in the quicksand of a crisis, remember that it is not a sign of weakness to reach out and call for help. In fact, calling for someone to throw you a lifeline may be the only way to free yourself from your predicament. Having at least one person available for such emotional lifesaving duties should become one of your personal survival priorities.

For many of us, the problem is not knowing whom to call on in such situations. It is not unusual for people to be reluctant to confide and entrust their most intimate problems and emotions to just anyone. This is certainly understandable. However, some of us are so afraid of the risks involved in disclosure and intimacy that we refuse to permit anyone to get close enough to know the real issues and emotions that are tearing apart and shredding our inner fabric. Ironically, even those of us who are married sometimes conceal the essence of our personhood from our own spouses.

Let's examine, for a moment, what might account for some of us playing life so "close to the vest" that we keep our emotional distance from everyone, even perhaps our mate. From early infancy through adulthood, we strive for acceptance and seek to avoid rejection. Acceptance and/or approval can take many forms. A smile, a touch, some words of affection all evoke a feeling of security and well-being. When you feel accepted in a relationship or situation, then you feel freer to interact, experience, explore and risk, more fully, the dynamics and potential of that relationship. However, unless and until you are confident that such acceptance has been achieved, you are often preoccupied with securing that feeling of approval. Other aspects of the relationship are usually subordinated to achieving your primary goal of acceptance. In essence, if your behaviors are governed by an overriding need and desire to be well liked by those with whom you have interactions, then you may reason that you cannot afford to let them know what you really think, feeling that it might compromise your image or cast you in a less than favorable light.

Unless and until that acceptance is achieved, you may build and maintain walls and moats to keep the "invaders" from finding out your innermost fears, anxieties, hopes, aspirations, fantasies and dreams. Don't let them penetrate your wall or cross your moat! Don't let them find out the real you! If you do, you reason, you may be hurt, betrayed and or rejected. To follow this faulty logic to its conclusion, you therefore must not share those intimate, unsettling feelings that may be tearing you apart. You feel obligated to leave untarnished and continue to project your facade of a happy, "together" personality.

The crux of the problem often lies in our inability or unwillingness to differentiate "invaders" from "allies." Each person you meet and know should earn the right, based on your judgment, to some level of penetration into your emotional fortress. You must find one, two or three such people with whom to share your confidence. These people should be seen as allies, not invaders. Now, it is true that just like the "Trojan horse" story, you may occasionally be deceived by invaders who may present themselves as allies. They pretend to be your friend while in fact they are knifing you in the back. However, you can survive such a deception, learn from it and next time be more selective about whom you choose to confide in. Don't overreact to such betrayals by resorting to an isolationist philosophy. The real "allies" in your life will accept you for who you are, including your warts, blemishes, idiosyncrasies, bad breath and faults. They are the ones you call on when you're drowning. They are the lifeguards of your life.

However, wanting and expecting total, unequivocal acceptance from all people is not only unrealistic but it is also undesirable! Do you want to bend yourself into a pretzel, trying never to offend, always accommodating, always double thinking, just to assure acceptance? It requires too much work, too much expenditure of energy, and results in too much self-resentment for being untrue to your true feelings, values and beliefs. In short, it reduces you to an emotional prostitute, selling your soul for approval. Yes, we all make accommodations and compromises to please others, but when it becomes obsessive and compulsive, then it also becomes repulsive!

To varying degrees, this is true for many of us. At one extreme is the person who is obsessed by being liked by everyone, at all times, forever. Such a person is destined to be endlessly frustrated and insecure. On the other end of the continuum is the person who sends out the message, "Take me or leave me—but I'm going to follow my own drumbeat." As in most examples of extremes, both are fraught with problems. Fortunately most of us fall somewhere in the middle. However, in the context of the importance of sharing one's feelings with others, it is clear that those individuals who are programmed for approval are deprived of the opportunity to unload and share their emotional burdens with others. To do so might result, so they think, in rejection.

However, I have observed that, though it may not have come easily, those who take the risk and reveal their feelings to selected others are not only accepted but they in fact receive a level of acceptance and approval that are deeper and more satisfying than what they imagined or experienced before. Indeed, such sharing and intimacy can become habit forming.

The flip side, then, is to understand the significant role you can play for another person if she selects you to be her confidant. To effectively fill that role, be a good listener, try to be non-judgmental, ask clarifying questions, give eye contact and, most important, respect confidentiality. As the poet John Donne said, "No man is an island." We all need to have allies and to be an ally to others.

PRESCRIPTION NO. 24

Allow selected people into your inner defenses

- From time to time, everyone needs a shoulder to cry on.

- Don't let your pride or preoccupation with being accepted or rejected get in the way of letting your hair down with someone you trust.

- Learn to differentiate between an invader and an ally.

- Share your confidences with others, and be there for others when they need you.

- It's better to be double-crossed or rejected than not to have the benefit of a confidant.

CHAPTER 25

Who Can You Count On and Who Can Count On You?

In order to achieve your dreams and goals, you must recognize that you cannot do it alone. No matter how much desire, drive, talent, skill or creativity you may possess, in most instances you will need to depend on other people to assist you. As stated in the last chapter, there is much truth to John Donne's words, "No man is an island."

Although you can hire and pay for help, it has been my experience that some of the most meaningful and valuable support one can receive is given by people you know who deeply care for you as a person, who believe in your abilities and who sincerely want you to succeed. That kind of help and support cannot be bought. It is priceless.

Regardless of how confident you may be, there are periods of loneliness, anxiety, second thoughts and apprehension when you are taking personal, professional and/or financial risks in pursuit of your goals and ambitions. At such times, the need for and importance of moral and emotional support is critical. Knowing that you have a "cheering section" and an emotional "safety net" to reinforce your confidence and determination is indispensable. However, none of us can just assume that such support will automatically be available and forthcoming from others. It either has or has not developed and evolved over time. The adages "what you send out is what you get back" and "you must be a friend to have a friend" are both true. Emotionally normal and stable people don't want to live in a vacuum. They need and want other people. They want human interaction.

Trying to accomplish a goal without the assistance of others is difficult in itself, but achieving a goal without having people you care about around you to share in your triumph and success is even more difficult. Life has purpose and meaning when it can be shared with others; otherwise one is left with lonely victories and meaningless successes. So creating, nurturing and maintaining close relationships with people you care about should be an ongoing activity. Being there to support and share with others, during both good and bad times, because you truly care for and about them, is important. Your motives for doing so should not be the expectation of reciprocation from the other party. *The emphasis should be on the giving, not the getting.* Your motivation should be the fantastic, exhilarating feelings that come from helping and being close with another human being, though a natural byproduct of your giving is hopefully the love that you will receive back from others. It is critical that each of us understands, appreciates and practices this principle of interdependence. The form and quantity of support you will receive from another will vary, but the sincerity and motivation should be obvious.

Have you ever thought about who are the people in your life for whom, if needed, you would drop what you are doing and run to be at their side? Who do you think would come to you if you called or needed them? Respond to the two Interdependence Inventory sheets to see if there are any surprises.

INTERDEPENDENCE INVENTORY #1

List the names of at least six people (at least two who are not family members) for whom you would, if called upon, immediately stop what you are doing and be available for them in their time of crisis, any hour, day or night.

_____

_____

_____

_____

_____

_____

Which of the following types of support would you be willing to give these people?

_____ Spend, with them whatever time they needed
_____ Give or loan them money even if it might strain your bank account

____ Let them indefinitely move into your home
____ Sacrifice a very special vacation to be with them
____ Share a very personal secret that might help them with their problem
____ Donate a kidney
____ Other

INTERDEPENDENCE INVENTORY #2

List the names of at least six people (at least two who are not family members) who you believe would immediately stop what they were doing and be available for you in your time of crisis, any hour of the day or night.

_____

_____

_____

_____

_____

_____

Which of the following do you think they would be willing to do for you?

_____ Spend with you whatever time you needed

_____ Give or loan you money even if it might strain their bank account

_____ Let you move indefinitely into their home

_____ Sacrifice a very special vacation to be with you

_____ Share a very personal secret that might help you with your problem

_____ Donate a kidney

_____ Other

Upon completion did you find the same names on both lists? If not, why not?

Now, if you really want to take this activity to the next level, ask those people you put on your list to create their own list and see if you are on it.

Given that we need human interaction, the questions then become how many people do you need, how much and how often is the interaction you want and need, and how intimate is the relationship you desire. The saying that most of us have many acquaintances and a few real friends is pretty accurate. Be sure that you have positioned yourself to be an acquaintance to many people and a real friend to at least a few. Also keep in mind the old expression, "Be nice to people on the way up because you never know whom you will meet on the way down." **The real question to ask yourself is: Whom you can count on and who can count on you?**

PRESCRIPTION NO. 25

Know whom you can count on and who can count on you

- Don't live your life as a "loner."

- Identify at least two or three people whom you can depend on in a time of crisis.

- Ask them to be a part of your support team.

- Offer to be a part of their support team.

CHAPTER 26

Getting Traded Can Be a Good Thing!

One of the accepted truths about professional sports in any country is that any player, regardless of his tenure or level of performance, is subject to being traded by the team's management. Even the great American baseball icon Babe Ruth was traded from the Boston Red Sox to the New York Yankees. (What were they thinking?) Sometimes trades work out for teams, sometimes only one team benefits and occasionally both teams find, after the fact, that they made a mistake. The decision to trade a player is usually motivated by several considerations. A team may be disappointed in the performance of the player; the player may no longer fit into the style of play the team wishes to pursue; another player, who is perceived as being more talented, becomes available; a player's behavior may negatively affect the chemistry on the team; budgetary constraints make the player a poor fit, and the list goes on.

If any of these issues come into play, then the team either releases a player outright or seeks a trade with another team. It does not and cannot permit itself to consider the personal impact such a trade may have on the player or his family: whether the player must move to another city, the possible loss of income, diminished playing time, or even the end of his career. The team's management is simply making a business decision that it is obligated to make.

Well, in the non-sports world, many of you who are not professional athletes are subject to being "traded" or "released" as well. Some of you are "traded" or "released" out of a marriage by your spouse, some of you are "released" by being fired from a job and some of you are "traded" by a social group or organization that no longer invites you to its functions. Whether it is your spouse, your boss, a friend or an association board, they, like the management of a sports team, have determined that they no longer wish to continue an association with you. They, too, may not be concerned about the personal impact their decision will have on your life.

However, you and the professional athlete have something in common. You are both human beings with feelings and emotions. You are both likely to feel a significant letdown or depression when confronted with the reality of being "traded" or "released." No matter what the reason, you feel rejected. If you choose to interpret it that way, you might indeed see it as rejection, but the key word for you to think about is "choose." You and the professional athlete can *choose* to feel that you have in some way failed or disappointed yourself or the other party. You can choose to feel that your sense of self worth has been diminished. You can choose to feel and act like a victim.

Or you can choose to analyze your situation in terms that will be more helpful to you and allow you to move forward.

The only reality is that there has been a parting of the ways between you and someone else or another entity. That this parting of ways was initiated by them is the only established, objective fact that is not subject to interpretation. Anything else that is attributed to the situation is subjective and open for interpretation

I recommend that you recognize and focus on the objective facts and then consider some positive things that can also happen to a player who is traded. He often finds:

- His new team is a better fit
- Under a new coach, with new teammates, in a new organization, his enthusiasm is rekindled, and this can renew the player's enthusiasm.
- His performance is often better with the new team. In hindsight, he may even wish that he had been traded or released sooner.
- He is **happier, happier, happier!**

This is not always the scenario, but it can be and often is.

If your marriage has dissolved, if you have lost your job, if you are no longer included in a social or professional group, then here are some steps to follow:

1. Think of yourself as a professional athlete who has just been traded or released.
2. Initially just define the situation in objective terms: "The other party initiated a parting of the ways with me for reasons that made sense to them."
3. Remember that this parting has not in any way affected

your knowledge and your talents or the essence of who you are as a person.

4. Ask yourself, "Is there anything I can learn from this situation that can help me be a better person in the future?"

5. Spin the situation to your advantage by seeing yourself with an opportunity to find a better "team" to "play for."

6. As quickly as possible, harness and focus your energies toward moving forward with your life

Remember, the team that traded you may have done you a big favor. It saw something that you didn't see or that you didn't want to see. It created an opportunity for you to move forward not because you are a "reject" but because you are a "great prospect" for another team. Go make the team that released you feel like the Boston Red Sox have felt for decades, since trading Babe Ruth to the Yankees. What a mistake!! Make the team that traded you feel like the Atlanta Falcons football team has felt ever since they released a young quarterback named Brett Favre. He has become been one of the greatest quarterbacks in the history of football while playing for the Green Bay Packers, and he will soon be headed to the Football Hall of Fame. The Falcons are still kicking themselves.

So if you are "traded" at any time in your life, be sure to "spin" the trade into a winning situation for you. You can do that if you handle it like the winner you are.

PRESCRIPTION NO. 26

If you are ever "traded," treat it as an opportunity, not a rejection

- Being "traded" or "released" is a decision made by someone else because he perceived it as being the right thing to do at the time.

- He has a right to make that decision.

- Put a positive "spin" on the situation.

- You have the choice to turn that decision into a wonderful opportunity for yourself. Remember the "Babe!"

- And remember, happiness is an attitude.

CHAPTER 27

Communication:
The Buck Stops with You!

"IT'S ALL YOUR FAULT!" "IT'S NEVER MY FAULT!" So often, we cannot resist the temptation to project outward, onto others, responsibility and blame for our unhappiness, shortcomings and dissatisfaction with our life. Let's start with the government at the national, state and local levels, which provides us with a terrific "whipping boy" for blaming all of the economic and political unhappiness that impact our lives. Of course, our boss at work takes the blame for all the job-related stress we experience. Let's not forget that sourpuss of a store clerk who will not accept, without a sales receipt, your purchase for return and refund. She is also available to serve as a dumpster for all the frustration you encounter dealing with the bureaucratic mentality. Finally there are those you love most, your spouse, children, parents and other close family members and friends who frequently receive sometimes a fair and sometimes an inordinate share of your generalized anger, frustration and anxiety.

In each instance, the tendency is perhaps for you *not* to consciously confront the real source of the negative feelings that reside within you. Rather, you may resort to tactics and responses of displaced anger that say to those around you, "You are the culprit making me feel so lousy, and I'm going to let you know, loud and clear, how much I resent your behavior." However, remember that when you point a finger at someone else, you may have three pointing back at you. Therefore, before you put the spotlight and microscope on the other person(s), take a look at your own needs, idiosyncrasies and tolerance levels to understand your role and responsibility in the dynamics of a situation. It really takes an adult mindset to do this. If you want to really begin improving your relationships, then stop projecting outward and start looking inward.

Sociologists refer to people as being either "internalists" or "externalists." Internalists look inward, to themselves for explanations and responsibility for why things happen in their life. Externalists, on the other hand, look outward to find blame in others or external circumstances for their lot in life. Do you see yourself as an internalist or externalist type personality?

The truth of the matter is that in relationships and interactions between and among people a chemical reaction occurs that results in either a stable or highly volatile mixture. The cliché, "It takes two to tango," deserves reflection in this case. So much of the solution to many of your problems resides in your ability to effectively communicate the things you like, the things you don't like, the things you want and the things you need. This requires an understanding of certain verbal and listening skills and your ability to use them.

It is impossible for one person to start an argument without the tacit or complete cooperation of at least one other party. There is no point in Person A ranting and raving unless Person B is aware of those behaviors and feelings. Without that knowledge, the most that Person A can accomplish is "stewing in her own juices." Person A is deprived of any satisfaction. It's like the old question, "If a tree falls in a forest and nobody is there, does it make a noise?" We can assume it does, but there is no substitute for someone being present to hear it. Therefore at least two parties must consent to participate in the "dance of anger."

For example, let's say you have had an unusually rough day at the office. You come home to find that your spouse does not have your dinner ready. Normally you would exhibit patience and keep yourself occupied until the meal is ready, or perhaps you could even help make it yourself. But on this night you are so pent up with anger that this delay with dinner just triggers a response that under normal circumstances you, yourself, would consider inappropriate.

You not only angrily complain about the dinner not being ready, you also expand and generalize about how this is typical of your spouse's shoddy and uncaring behavior. "Since you have nothing to do but take care of the house and kids all day while I, bust my gut out there in the 'jungle,' the least you could do is have dinner ready on time! I guess I shouldn't be so surprised, since you never seem to care or try to understand the pressures I'm under."—and now for the ultimate salvo—"You're just like your mother!" Let the games begin!! The gauntlet has been dropped, and the war has begun.

A typical spouse who is not knowledgeable in the art of listening and hearing the feelings of anger and fatigue would probably respond to this verbal assault with a "knee-jerk" reaction of, "Oh yeah? Well, if you don't like the way I'm doing things around here you can take your dinner and . . ." At this point, you and your spouse have set the stage for an evening of hostility, unhappiness and distance between yourselves. A cauldron of hurt and angry feelings is bubbling to a boil. Your inability to identify and control your displaced anger, which developed at work, has now begun to create a "snowball effect" of unhappiness for you in other areas of your life.

How can this fallout from your "anger bomb" be avoided? Clearly the answer is not to deny or even to repress your feelings of anger. To do so, might lead to a festering and exacerbation of your anger that would either result in a delayed explosion and/or some physical illness, such as headaches, ulcers, high blood pressure, stroke, etc. The best solution depends on your own willingness and ability to tune in to your own feelings and to identify those feelings and their origin. This is easier said than done. However, by making a conscious effort to ask yourself the questions, "What feelings am I feeling? What caused them? How can I best deal with them?" you can, with practice, begin to resist the temptation to project those feelings onto innocent bystanders.

Another very valuable approach to this situation is for you and those closest to you to learn the skill of "reflective listening." There are several good books and courses available that can teach you this skill, which basically involves the ability to not only listen but also to *hear* the feelings and emotions people express in their verbal statements. Once you, as the listener, think you have identified the feeling being conveyed, you should respond to the sender using a "feeling word phrase" that will let the sender know you really heard the emotion in her message. It's only after the other party knows from your response that you heard her feelings that you can proceed to deal with the substance of the message

Let's go back to our earlier scenario where one spouse said to the other, "I guess I shouldn't be so surprised, since you never seem to care or understand the pressures I'm under." A non -reflective response might be, "Well, I'm under plenty of pressures too! You think it's easy being home all day?" (or ". . . holding a job and then coming home to make dinner?") Notice how the listener totally ignored the feeling contained in the message received, and instead becomes caught up in conveying her *own* feelings of being pressured.

A reflective response might be, "You really feel that I don't understand and that I am not concerned with the feelings of stress that you experience every day, huh?" The "huh" at the end is very important, since it invites the other party to respond by either acknowledging that she was heard and/or by encouraging further clarification and information.

The value of using reflective listening responses with others is to lower the likelihood of unnecessary confrontation and to increase clear communication, which can result in conflict reduction. Can you think of times when you've said something and you felt that your message was ignored? How did you feel? You probably felt frustrated and angry. When you receive non-reflective responses, it tends to heighten your level of emotion and impedes and distorts your ability to discuss the issue in a rational manner.

Many of us are not good listeners. There is a tendency to be so absorbed in yourself, in your own thoughts, that in conversations your mind becomes preoccupied with what you plan to say. Rather than in really listening to what someone else is saying, you can't wait to interrupt or find an opening to inject your own thoughts and feelings. You need to recognize the difference between the act of hearing and the act of listening.

Hearing is a passive activity. Listening is an active process. It takes a great deal of hard work to concentrate and to listen. Listening often requires that you do several things at the same time. In addition to listening to the words, a good listener is also sensitive to picking up the emotion behind those words and the nonverbal body language that accompanies the message. An exceptional listener is also aware of her own frame of mind and her attitude toward the speaker and the subject being discussed, and how it might affect the processing and interpretation of the message.

It's not unusual to find a lack of consistency between the verbal words being spoken and the body language being used. Have you ever been told by someone, "Yes, yes, do it if you feel it's that important," while their nonverbal body language was sending off signals that said, "I really don't want you to do it"? It's very confusing to the listener to determine what the person is really saying. Therefore be sure that your body language, tone of voice and the words you speak are all in sync.

Breakdowns in government and business negotiations and the deterioration of personal relationships are often attributed to poor communications. President Lyndon B. Johnson popularized the phrase, "What we have here is a failure to communicate." If, in fact, communication is so vital to maintaining most relationships, and it is, then why don't you and I do a better job at sending and receiving messages?

Perhaps part of the answer is that either we are not really interested in what the other party has to say and/or we see many conversations as a competitive event, in which our primary objective is to score "points." If the problem is lack of interest or concern for the other party and her feelings, then the relationship is probably doomed to failure or at the very least it will function on a very superficial level. People or groups that don't value each other's thoughts, feelings or concerns tend to hear each other, but they do not listen. They tend to *talk at* each other rather than to *speak with* each other. Being willing to listen attentively to another person is truly one of the most valuable gifts you can give that person. It is an act of unselfishness.

So, too, people or groups that, either on a conscious or subconscious level, feel a sense of competitiveness or a struggle for power or control frequently become more preoccupied with "scoring points" and being "right" in their conversations with others than on really communicating or solving a problem. If your game is to score points, then the tendency in conversations is for you to devote your energies to thinking about your own point of view rather than to listening to what the other party is saying.

Recognize the role that effective communication techniques, including speaking and listening skills, can have on improving your relationships. What is important is to listen to each other. Be willing to accept responsibility for seeing that the communication is successful—not necessarily that you agree but that you truly have understood each other.

PRESCRIPTION NO. 27

Accept 51% of the responsibility for making a communication work

- Be willing to work harder than the other party.

- Be a reflective listener.

- Speak rather than talk.

- Observe rather than see.

- Listen rather than hear.

- The buck stops with you!

CHAPTER 28

Take a Lesson from Julia and Denzel

Have you ever wondered how movie, TV or stage actors or actresses manage to deliver convincing, award-winning, consistent performances night after night, show after show? Wouldn't you expect them to wear down, let down, get lax or in some way deliver less than what the audience expects? After all, what we, their fan base, their audience tend to forget is that actors and actresses are real people with real lives and real problems. Take away the fame and the money and they are made of blood, flesh and bones, just like you. These folks have their share of marital woes (make that more than their share), but when the lights go on and the camera is rolling, their training kicks in and they are charming, glib and entertaining. If the role calls for them to be scary, then they can make us scream in fear. If the role calls for humor, then they can make us laugh and squeal with delight. They can manipulate our emotions with seemingly effortless behavior.

So how do they manage to set aside or conceal all the distractions, pain and conflict that are hammering their real lives? The answer is pretty self-evident: They are trained, professional actors and actresses. They know how to shed one character and take on the persona, psyche and essence of another character. They have learned how to temporarily lose them-selves and become a fictional character. The fact remains, how-ever, that in reality they are not immune or insulated from the same issues that you and I contend with every day.

So what can Julia Roberts and Denzel Washington teach us? To be an actor or an actress in life. Your audience, your family, your friends, your co-workers and acquaintances do not want to hear every gruesome detail about your life. They don't always want to be dragged in and dragged down to the depths of your despair. There are times when someone greets you with the habitual, "How's it going?" that he really doesn't want a true answer. Recognize and spare him the ordeal of "dumping" your frustrations and problems on him. On a sub-conscious level, many of these people want you to act and pre-tend. They want you to give them the scripted answer, "Every-thing is great."

There is a rather interesting concept that says that when two people, each with an opposite frame of mind, meet each other, whichever person is more committed to his frame of mind will usually bring the other person in his direction. So hypothetically, if we meet and I am optimistic and happy and you are pessimistic and sad, then at the end of our meeting either I will leave feeling like you or you will leave feeling like me. It is a subconscious battle of wills to our respective frame of mind. Obviously, you and I would prefer to be around posi-tive thinking and acting people. Rather than relying on the other party to lift you up, why not make a conscious effort to be the one positively impacting others? If you do, you will probably find that people will seek you out as opposed to avoiding your negative karma. Remember, "Laugh and the world laughs with you, cry and you cry alone."

Let's think about the implications of "acting" in a very practical context: Let's say you lose your job. You are emotionally and financially devastated. What are you to do? How will you find another job that pays as much and that you will like? The more time that elapses during the job search, the more your confidence wanes. You become depressed, you become anxious, and a feeling of desperation begins to hover over your life. When you do get a job interview, you interview badly and don't get the job. The prospective employer is not meeting a confident, competent you; she is meeting a basket case dressed in a suit and tie or skirt and jacket. You're lost before you begin. You are sending out negative vibes that say, "I'm a loser." Who wants to invest in a "basket case," in "a head case," in someone who will drain the employer's time and energy?

So what's a fellow or gal to do? **Act! Act! Act!** Consciously conceal your negativity and self-doubt and learn the script that conveys optimism and competence. Dress and act the part of a winner. Employers want to hire winners. The sooner you learn how to "act," the faster you will find a new position.

Is there anything immoral or unethical if you embrace this acting philosophy? Absolutely not! This is a pragmatic coping mechanism to enable you to be better for yourself and others. To paraphrase William Shakespeare, life is a stage and we are merely the players. Master the art of acting, and you will become empowered to distance yourself from your problems. Sometimes this distance will give you time to get a better handle on your available options.

Acting does have its limitations. It's an issue of degree and frequency. There are times to be an actor, and there are times to let your hair down. You have to find the right balance between playing the role of the stoic martyr who always suffers in silence, which I am definitely not advocating, and, on the other extreme, being a constant whiner and complainer.

Note: I do not mean to suggest that there aren't selected people in whom you should confide. I just want to remind you that putting on a brave face is sometimes in your, and others', best interest. Ask yourself: Can I benefit from acting lessons in my life? When appropriate, are my acting skills good enough to get me an Academy Award nomination in the category of "Best Actor/Actress in a real life situation where it was in my and others' best interest to put on a happy face?"

PRESCRIPTION NO. 28

When the situation calls for it, be an actor or an actress

- When professional actors and actresses are in character, both you and they forget about their personal problems.

- Play a leading role in your life: the part of a person who is really happy and optimistic.

- Masking your feelings on occasion may be a good thing.

- It's a matter of not overdoing the acting and not getting typecast as a "complainer" or a "martyr."

- Know when to act and when to be real.

CHAPTER 29

Enjoy Yourself,
It's Later Than You Think

Both my grandfathers were immigrants from Eastern Europe and struggled their way from the poverty ghettos of the Lower East Side of New York to eventual middle- class status in the Bronx and Brooklyn. Although I have many warm, beautiful memories of these two wonderful men, who are both deceased, the most vivid memory that they etched in my heart was the favorite song that they each would sing with zest and gusto.

Grandpa Izzy frequently sang a Yiddish song called "Ich Daf a Bissel Mazel," whose words in English are, roughly translated, "To get through life I need a little luck and a lot of inner strength." You may be familiar with my Grandpa Max's theme song, an American one entitled, "Enjoy Yourself (It's Later Than You Think)" by Herbert Magidson and Carl Sigman. The words of the song encourages you to enjoy your life while you are still healthy and before life passes you by, because the years pass "as quickly as a wink."

The thoughts expressed in both of these songs embrace the essence of much of my philosophy of life. By sharing these songs with you, I want you to think about the wisdom in the words of each of these songs as you review your own song of life. Yes, I believe that each of us should have a personal song of life. As we walk through the "minefield" of life, each of us should have one or two songs, pieces of philosophy, or spiritual beliefs that serve to anchor us against the emotional blasts that periodically occur when we step on one of life's mines.

Many of the talks that I give to public, private and business organizations revolve around the theme of how to make the most out of one's life. The desire to make life satisfying and fulfilling is shared by people from all walks of life. Presidents of corporations, blue-collar workers, males, females, people of all races, creeds and nationalities all want basically the same thing: *happiness and peace of mind.*

In fact, people spend billions of dollars each year on trips, clothes, houses, cars, pills, psychiatrists and even motivational speakers in the hope of attaining these goals. The truth of the matter is that happiness and peace of mind are not absolutes that can be captured, placed in a jar and carried around throughout your life. Clearly they are a function of your state of mind and circumstances, and they occur, to varying degrees, at different times in your life. The most important thing is to identify and recognize what really makes you happy. Each of us has a different yardstick to define and measure happiness, which is as it should be. There is no right or wrong, good or bad when it comes to happiness, provided that your decisions are in sync with and do not harm the people in your life who are affected by those decisions.

The basic message of this book, as it relates to your life, can best be restated and summarized by recalling the parable about the Wise Man who was reputed to know the answer to every question. One day a boy approached him and asked, "Wise man, if you are so smart, answer this: I have a bird in my hand. Is it alive or dead?" The wise man answered, "My son, if I say the bird is alive, then you will crush it with your fingers and kill it; if I say it is dead, you will open your fingers and prove that it is alive. So you see, my son, it is what you will it to be."

To a large degree, dear reader, your future happiness and contentment, your life story is **what you will it to be!** Whatever it is that you ultimately decide to pursue as your goals for happiness, I encourage you to remember my Grandpa Izzy and Grandpa Max. Accept and be grateful when you are the recipient of the kind hand of fate, lady luck. Someone is going to win the lottery, but the odds are it won't be you. Don't depend on luck. **Make your own luck!** Depend on your own inner strength, and be sure to enjoy each moment, each relationship, each experience and each opportunity because, as my Grandpa Max would say, "It's later than you think."

Have a personal guiding principle to anchor your life

- Select a song, religious or moral principle.

- Use it as your guide and anchor in making decisions.

- Take responsibility for improving your life.

- You have the power. Use it!

A Review of Dr. Fred's Practical Prescriptions for Happiness

Do it now! Say it now! Enjoy it now!

- Don't assume you will have a tomorrow to reconcile with a loved one, to attend your child's recital, to whisper a word of tenderness, love or encouragement, to take that trip, to make that telephone call, to make amends.
- You are only guaranteed this moment. Make the most of it!
- Embrace a mindset of urgency, curiosity, interest and appreciation for the opportunity to be alive.
- Don't take people, experiences or time for granted. As the song from the play *La Cage Aux Folles* says, "The best of times is now!"

Make your decisions based on reality, not fantasy

- Abstractions are great in the world of art, but use concrete, realistic reasoning when making decisions in your personal life.
- Be honest with yourself and others, even if you don't like what you see.
- Determine how badly you want something and what sacrifices you are willing to make to get it. If the clarity and passion are not present, then, for now, pass on it.
- Don't beat yourself up over your decision. Accept it and move on.

PRESCRIPTION NO. 3

Set high goals and force yourself to stretch

- Don't underestimate your abilities or those of others.
- No matter how hard you try and how much you achieve, you can still try harder and go farther if you **stretch**.
- Remember the saying, "If you reach for the sky, you won't end up with a handful of mud."

PRESCRIPTION NO. 4

Think and act like a motivated immigrant

- You are a member of the lucky minority on this planet.
- You really have few excuses to fall back on.
- Don't squander your good fortune. "Go for the gold."
- To realize your dreams and aspirations, think, act and sacrifice as if you were an immigrant to this country.

PRESCRIPTION NO. 5

Squeeze your "orange of life" with all your might!

- Think of your life as a big orange waiting to be squeezed.
- The amount of time, energy and effort you expend in squeezing will determine the amount of "juice" in your cup.
- Make sure your hand aches so your cup will "runneth over."

PRESCRIPTION NO. 6

Define what you want out of life

- In the book *Alice in Wonderland* is the famous line, "If you don't know where you are going, then any road will get you there."
- Periodically, call time out from your treadmill.
- Review, revisit, re-evaluate your values and goals before getting back on.

PRESCRIPTION NO. 7

Each day, spin only your priority "plates"

- The "Law of the Spinning Plates" is grounded in common sense.
- Accept the physical, emotional and time limitations you have on how many "plates" you can realistically spin at any one time.
- Each day, decide to focus your energies and time on your priority plates and spin the others when you can.
- The life you save may be your own!

PRESCRIPTION NO. 8

When making decisions, use your "minesweepers"

- Experience, intuition and self-awareness are some of the "minesweepers" that will minimize the number of times that you step on one of life's mines. Listen to those minesweepers even if you don't like what they are saying.
- Stepping on a mine from time to time is normal and inevitable but is seldom fatal.
- Learn from the experience.
- Keep moving forward, and don't let fear of life's mines immobilize you.

PRESCRIPTION NO. 9

Take risks as often as you can

- The greatest risk in life is not taking a risk. You will never know what you could have had or experienced.
- Take more risks and experience the exhilaration of really feeling alive. It beats the boredom of security and predictability.
- So what if you make a mistake? Most situations are reversible.
- Remember the saying, "You can't get to second base until you take your foot off of first base."

PRESCRIPTION NO. 10

Don't take your life and loved ones for granted

- Every day, through your decisions and actions, you put a "price" on how much you value the people in your life.
- Don't wait for an unexpected "rain" or tragic turn of events to remind you that you may have undervalued your relationships.
- While the sun is still shining, tell your loved ones you love them.

PRESCRIPTION NO. 11

Be honest with yourself in appraising situations

- Have the courage to recognize that part of your life may not be as "clothed" as you would like.
- Recognizing your "nakedness" is the beginning of true growth and development.
- Accept the truth and use it as the foundation for building your relationships and making your decisions.

PRESCRIPTION NO. 12

Take responsibility for your life

- Your future and your fortune cannot be found in a fortune cookie someone else has baked.
- Be the baker, determine the type of good fortune you want, secure the ingredients, mix the batter and then bake on high motivation and commitment for the rest of your life.
- You must provide the MSG: Motivation, Sacrifice and Grit! It will improve the taste of your life!

Don't Be a Captive of "Golden Handcuffs"

- "Golden handcuffs" are made of emotion, not steel.
- They are tempered by fear of the unknown and by uncertainty and doubt.
- The key to unlock them is made of reason, self-honesty and hope.
- Have the courage to turn the key.
- Remember, there is a difference between real gold and "fool's gold."

Use a positive attitude and common sense to get out of a "slump"

- Keep in perspective what is really going on in your life.
- Be a player, not a spectator.
- Some good things and some bad things will happen during the game.
- Be grateful for the opportunity to play.
- Improve your attitude, take a step back, analyze what's causing the slump and address the source of the problem.
- Sometimes you *will* need to consult a "coach."

React to each adversity in proportion to its severity

- There is a definite difference between a disappointment, a setback and a tragedy. The depth and intensity of your response should reflect the reality of each situation.
- Evaluate the situation objectively.

- Don't overreact.
- Adopt a "survivor" mentality.
- After adversity, move forward with your life as quickly as possible. *What's the alternative?*

PRESCRIPTION NO. 16

Monitor and respond to your dashboard of life

- You were given the gift of dashboard lights in your life.
- To avoid breaking down on your highway of life, monitor them and heed them.
- Keep your eyes focused more on your dashboard and less on your accelerator.

PRESCRIPTION NO. 17

Choose the octane level that you need to get where you want to go

- Decide where you want to go.
- Determine how you plan to get there.
- Identify the level of "octane" you need, and know where to find the gas pump.
- Be sure you can afford the fill-up.

PRESCRIPTION NO. 18

Ride as many rides as possible in the amusement park of life

- Ride all the rides in the "Amusement Park of Life."
- Each ride will help you to achieve a different goal.

- Make sure that you're emotionally old enough and healthy enough for the rides you select.
- Don't limit yourself to the safe, familiar merry-go-round.
- Allow yourself to experience the fear, the fun, the rush of new rides.

PRESCRIPTION NO. 19

Increase your tolerance for sacrifice to achieve what you want

- Life works on the "pleasure-pain principle."
- If you want something badly enough, then you'll endure the pain.
- You have a higher "pain threshold" than you think.
- Be honest with yourself as to what you really want and how badly you want it. The motivation will follow.
- Never begrudge others their successes. They earned it.
- Be like Farmer Brown and be willing to milk your cow.

PRESCRIPTION NO. 20

Toughen up! Use your inner strength as your adult "blankie"

- Whether you're eight months or eighty years old, it is normal to need and want a sense of security.
- As you get older, replace the tangible "blankie" you used as a child with your own personal emotional "blankie" made from memories of past accomplishments and recognition of your inherent worthiness as a human being.
- Remember ILAC: "I am lovable and capable."
- Come on, now—toughen up!

PRESCRIPTION NO. 21

Set deadlines for yourself

- There is a time to dream, but if you don't act on your dream by setting and meeting your deadlines, then your dream may become your nightmare or a mirage.
- Talk is cheap.
- Create structure, timelines, rewards and punishments to keep yourself on task.
- Understand the positive and negative consequences of what you do or don't do.

PRESCRIPTION NO. 22

Never give up! Never give up!

- Remind yourself how good you are.
- As long as there is life, there is hope, but hope alone is not enough. You must also act.
- You have the power to fight adversity.
- Either win or go down fighting.
- Surrender is for cowards.

PRESCRIPTION NO. 23

Confront and fight your fears

- If fear is your Goliath, then you must be the David. Take your slingshot, load up with rocks of belief in yourself and slay the giant!
- Your fear may not fall on the first shot, but over time you can wear it down.
- As big and scary as a fear may be in your mind, it is much less harmful to you than the feelings you will live with every day if you remain intimidated.

PRESCRIPTION NO. 24

Allow selected people into your inner defenses

- From time to time, everyone needs a shoulder to cry on.
- Don't let your pride or preoccupation with being accepted or rejected get in the way of letting your hair down with someone you trust.
- Learn to differentiate between an invader and an ally.
- Share your confidences with others, and be there for others when they need you.
- It's better to be double-crossed or rejected than not to have the benefit of a confidant.

PRESCRIPTION NO. 25

Know whom you can count on and who can count on you

- Don't live your life as a "loner."
- Identify at least two or three people whom you can depend on in a time of crisis.
- Ask them to be a part of your support team.
- Offer to be a part of their support team

PRESCRIPTION NO. 26

If you are ever "traded," treat it as an opportunity, not a rejection

- Being "traded" or "released" is a decision made by someone else because he perceived it as being the right thing to do at the time.
- He has a right to make that decision.
- Put a positive "spin" on the situation.
- You have the choice to turn that decision into a wonderful opportunity for yourself. Remember the "Babe!"
- And remember, happiness is an attitude.

PRESCRIPTION NO. 27

Accept 51% of the responsibility for making a communication work

- Be willing to work harder than the other party.
- Be a reflective listener.
- Speak rather than talk.
- Observe rather than see.
- Listen rather than hear.
- The buck stops with you!

PRESCRIPTION NO. 28

When the situation calls for it, be an actor or an actress

- When professional actors and actresses are in character, both you and they forget about their personal problems.
- Play a leading role in your life: the part of a person who is really happy and optimistic.
- Masking your feelings on occasion may be a good thing.
- It's a matter of not overdoing the acting and not getting typecast as a "complainer" or a "martyr."
- Know when to act and when to be real.

PRESCRIPTION NO. 29

Have a personal guiding principle to anchor your life

- Select a song, religious or moral principle.
- Use it as your guide and anchor in making decisions.
- Take responsibility for improving your life.
- You have the power. Use it!

A Closing Thought

Somewhat "tongue in cheek," the title of this book asks you if your life needs a laxative. In essence it suggests that perhaps some of the things you believe, say and do need to be replaced with other attitudes and behaviors that are more conducive to your happiness.

You've been provided a "buffet" of twenty-nine chapters and twenty-nine of Dr. Fred's Prescriptions for Happiness. If you went to a restaurant that served a buffet and attempted to eat everything available, you more than likely would get sick. So, too, I discourage you from embracing, accepting and applying every prescription that is provided in this book. Only some of them are applicable to your specific life situation. If you take just one or two ideas that you feel apply to you, then you will have truly benefited from this book and I will have achieved my purpose in writing it.

At different times in our lives each of us can be more vulnerable and susceptible to overreacting to an idea. This was once impressed upon me by an audience member who, in response to my advocacy of pursuing happiness, informed me at the end of a seminar, "Dr. Fred, I listened to you and I am going home and filing for a divorce." Although there was nothing in my comments that suggested or advocated divorce, this particular women was clearly overreacting prior to exploring other options. Fortunately she calmed down and, I am happy to report, is more happily married than ever. The point is to temper your reactions to the ideas that I've shared with you in this book with some reflective thought and discussion with others.

I also encourage you to periodically review the prescriptions at the end of the book. This will keep them at a conscious level in your mind and allow you to address those you think important.

It is my hope that you enjoyed the book and that you will be motivated to **act, act, act!** Until we meet again, remember: **Don't count your days, make your days count!**

About the Author

Fred Broder, Ph.D., is a guest lecturer for cruise lines such as Crystal, Holland America, Royal Olympic and Cunard. He is noted for his dynamic style of presentation that blends theatrics with practical, thought-provoking content. He has had his own motivational speaking, sales and management training and consulting business for more than eight years. His distinguished clients have included AirTran Airways, Kaiser Permanente, Bank of America, Bayer, Quaker Oats, Cox Communication, the Georgia Lottery, the *Atlanta Journal-Constitution*, the Social Security Administration, International Sanitary Supply Association, National Business Travel Association, Hank Aaron's 755 Corporation, Companion Casualty Insurance Company and Aaron Rents, just to name a few. In addition to his motivational speaking, Fred conducts skill development seminars in sales, management, customer service, communications, team building and strategic planning.

Fred holds a master's degree in administration/supervision and a doctorate in curriculum and instruction. He served as Director of Professional Development for an association of more than 35,000 members. Fred also served as Director of Organizational Development and Sales Training for a division of a Fortune 500 company with a sales force of 1,200 in forty branches throughout the U.S. and Canada.

Fred is married to Glenda and has three children: Eric, Jordy and Shira.

FOR MORE INFORMATION

To purchase additional copies (indicate if you
want the books dedicated and autographed)

or

for information on Fred Broder's group speaking
and training programs, call or write:

New Outlook Press
5369 Seaton Way Suite B
Atlanta, GA 30338
(770) 392-0382
fred@fredbroder.com

Visit Fred online: www.fredbroder.com